A PASSION FOR LEADERSHIP

Amazing results from a fabulous concept

A book about leading through positive energy

By Wayne Kehl

authorHOUSE

AuthorHouse™
1663 Liberty Drive, Suite 200
Bloomington, IN 47403
www.authorhouse.com
Phone: 1-800-839-8640

All characters appearing in this work are fictitious. Any resemblance to real persons, living or dead, is purely coincidental.

© 2008 Wayne Kehl. All rights reserved.

No part of this book may be reproduced, stored in a retrieval system, or transmitted by any means without the written permission of the author.

First published by AuthorHouse 5/12/2008

ISBN: 978-1-4343-7703-6 (sc)

Printed in the United States of America
Bloomington, Indiana

This book is printed on acid-free paper.

Contents

Foreword		vii
Introduction		ix
1.	I Hate This Place, But I Love My Paycheck	1
2.	Meet Walter Kennedy	9
3.	Positive Reinforcement	25
4.	That's Not My Job!	37
5.	Bosses Make Mistakes, Too	55
6.	Good Leaders Need Good Followeres	87
7.	A Positive Passion Presentation	119
8.	Personally Speaking	161
9.	The First Article: Self-Awareness	169
10.	Article Two: Management Disengagement - A Tragedy	179
11.	Article Three: Positive Consistency	193
12.	The Natural Tendency of Human Beings	203
Afterword		215

Foreword

You probably already know that the main reason employees leave companies is their personal feelings about their immediate supervisor. This wouldn't be that much of a problem except that with staffing shortages intensifying, managers can't afford to lose good people over personality differences. Unfortunately, few managers and supervisors have been equipped with the tools to address ***people problems***. Until now, that is.

In these pages, Wayne Kehl shares the secrets of how managers can not only correct problem behaviors, but also how to motivate and inspire these individuals to live up to their performance potential. And the bonus…as he did with his first book, Wayne has wrapped this message in a story format that makes **"A Passion for Leadership"** a pleasure to read.

You may be asking yourself, "Do these concepts really work?" The great thing I have gotten to know about Wayne while consulting with his management team is ***he walks his talk***. He is a senior manager in a successful organization and has tested these approaches in the living laboratory of his own company. These techniques work because they've been road tested. If you supervise, manage or inspire employees, this is the resource that you will turn to time and again.

Jeff Mowatt,
JC Mowatt Seminars Inc

Bestselling Author,
*Becoming a Service Icon
in 90 Minutes a Month*

Introduction

This is the second in a series of books that began with *Always Remember: If It Ain't Fun, It Ain't Worth Doing!* My first book chronicled the story of Walter Kennedy as he fought his way upstream in a river of management woes while attempting to always *do the right thing*. His failure as a manager was almost certain, but thanks to his friend, Joshua O'Hare, he was able to preserve his integrity and ended up taking over Joshua's successful tire business.

In this book we fast forward ten years to a forty-something Walter Kennedy who is the revered President and CEO of the fastest growing tire dealership in North America. He has taken on Joshua's dream of building the best tire business in the world and turned it into a reality. Despite the rapid growth of his firm, Walter stayed true to his beliefs and values while building his business on a foundation of fairness, compassion and open, honest communication. Joshua's Tire Center is an icon of employee satisfaction. While his competitors were cutting back on staff and reducing benefits, Walter's firm was growing, and his employees now enjoy the best benefits package and working conditions in the business. Joshua's Tires is not the highest paying firm of its kind, but it is the single most profitable, and it boasts a waiting list of thousands of prospective employee applications and résumés. It is the positive environment created by Joshua and nurtured by Walter that sets Joshua's Tires apart from all others.

Despite Walter's success at Joshua's Tires, there are problems. People will be people, and no matter how rigorous the employee selection process is, personalities will clash. In this book we again find Walter grappling with employee issues. This time it is different for Walter because in his position as President and CEO of this international tire business, he cannot possibly make time to deal with each and every employee or each and every problem. All he can do is observe, oversee the big picture, and make himself available to offer advice to his legion of managers.

Walter learned his management lessons well from Joshua, and he insists that his managers live and work by the same standards and values that he and Joshua did. He knows the value of good leadership. He has created an environment of trust and respect where fear does not exist and communication is king. His managers trust him and have no trepidation about coming to him with a problem. He is the epitome of a great leader, and he spends a good deal of time helping his good managers become great ones. He takes his responsibility one step further and strives to make his great managers into the greatest of leaders. Walter knows that we never stop learning and that perfection can never be achieved in a normal lifetime. Just when we think we have it right, something happens to prove us wrong.

In *A Passion for Leadership* we find out what toxic, negative employees are all about and how to handle them. We see how they directly and indirectly cause harm to the place they work. These people exist everywhere, and we all know some of them. Walter Kennedy has run up against a lot of them in his life, and although he doesn't always understand what drives them, he knows they must be dealt with before they have the opportunity to undermine the hard work of everyone else. Walter maintains an unwavering belief that through positive energy and positive action he can make a difference. He calls his belief ***positive passion.***

You will recognize co-workers, friends, loved ones and people you buy from on these pages. Toxic personalities are everywhere, and they are usually not exclusive to the workplace. As the chapters unfold, you will probably begin to realize that you, too, are working with toxic employees who have a need to make others unhappy, or at the very least, to unbalance them. These people often appear to want to destroy the credibility of their companies, its managers, and their co-workers, even at the risk of destroying their companies or losing their jobs.

Every workplace needs positive energy in order to succeed. Walter Kennedy's passion is to eliminate negativity and to impart positive energy wherever he can. He knows that as simple as this concept is, it is extremely difficult to get across to the vast majority of employees and managers. He also knows that it is *people* who create negativity in others and that only *people* can reverse the damage done by toxic employees. Walter knows the value of positive people, and when he finds them, he encourages and cultivates their motivating energy.

I hope you enjoy ***A Passion for Leadership*** and that you can bring the power of positive energy into your life.

CHAPTER ONE

I Hate This Place, But I Love My Paycheck

There are a number of people in the world who appear not to care about other people. Most of them don't mean it. You just need to touch the right chord in them...

CHAPTER 1

I Hate This Place, But I Love My Paycheck

Have you ever worked with someone you didn't like? Have you ever wondered why this person or that person was hired in the first place, or how they kept their jobs? Have you ever wished you could *destroy* one of your co-workers? Have you ever wanted to fire one of your top performers? Most human beings have negative thoughts about someone they work with from time to time.

Consider the story of Don, a salesman with Joshua's Tire Centers. He is a forty-year-old man with two kids and a wife. He and his family have a nice house and a summer cottage on a lake. He has two nice vehicles, a lot of grown-up toys and a six-figure income. Don is a good-looking guy with a lot of loyal clients and a great lifestyle. At first glance this man appears to have it all.

What problems could Don possibly have? In his own mind, he hasn't a problem in the world. In the mind of his boss and fellow employees, he is a disaster. At work, Don is a self centered, egotistical swine with a heart of stone. He routinely criticizes fellow employees behind their backs and to their faces. Don struts around the office with a smirk on his face just waiting for something to go wrong so he can point it out to everyone and blow it out of proportion. He constantly makes negative remarks about Joshua's Tire Centers and threatens to quit every time he doesn't get his own way. This is a guy nobody likes. To know him is to hate him. Co-workers wonder how he keeps his job.

Strangely, Don's clients love him, and he is one of Joshua's Tire Centers' best salesmen. Equally as strange, Don seems to genuinely care about his clients, and he is a model parent and husband. "How can he be so negative in some areas and so very positive in others?" his manager, Jim Balderson, mused to himself as he listened to one of his staff members complain about Don's attitude. The staff member, Jennifer, was the office accountant at the largest Joshua's Tire Shop in Vancouver.

"I have to tell you, Jim, Don is a total pain in the neck with everyone in the store. He is rude and obnoxious to every staff member we have here," Jennifer stated with conviction.

"I know, Jen," Jim said calmly. "Unfortunately, he is our top salesman, and his numbers so far this year are huge. We really have no choice but to put up with him."

Jen's eyes filled with tears as she began to tell Jim about how in front of customers at the front counter, Don told one of the girls, Carol, that if it weren't for her and her constant mistakes, Joshua's would have a lot more repeat customers.

"He didn't!" Jim gasped.

"He did!" Jen exclaimed.

"Oh, for God's sake, now I suppose I am going to have to have a chat with him and tell him to cool it again. I am getting so sick of this nonsense," Jim Balderson moaned.

Jim called Don on his direct line and asked him to come into his office.

"Sure, boss-man," Don chirped before hanging up the phone abruptly.

"So what's this I hear about you telling Carol that she makes too many mistakes?" Jim asked after Don had plunked himself down in the client chair in Jim's office.

"Well, she does," Don stated matter-of-factly while curling his lip and looking toward the floor.

"Cut the crap, Don. You can't talk that way about staff members in front of customers. In fact, you shouldn't talk about them that way at all!" Jim yelled.

"Well, if no one else around here is going to do anything about the incompetent employees we have in this place, then I guess it's up to me. God knows you never do anything about them!" Don said as he stared defiantly into Jim's eyes.

"There is nothing wrong with Carol. She is not incompetent, and she doesn't make any more mistakes than you do, Don. Leave her alone!" Jim said in an exasperated tone.

Don eyed Jim Balderson for a moment, sensing his anger. In a very cool tone he said, "Well, I might make a mistake or two, Jim, but I bring a lot more money into this place than Carol or anyone else out there. If you had more employees like me, you might make a success of this region."

Jim felt his face flush with anger. Even with his pulse racing, he was lucid enough to know that he couldn't afford to lose Don right now. The numbers in the office were in the black for the first time since the store had opened four years prior. Don was a field salesman who had a very large region to service. His sales numbers were among the best in the company and the thought of having him quit, or worse yet losing him to the competition, sent a shudder of fear through Jim Balderson's soul.

"Don, do me a favor and just stay off the radar, would you?" Jim asked patiently.

"Jim, I have nothing against you personally, but I make a lot of money for this company, and frankly, the only thing I ever hear is that I am the bad guy. I should be making way more money than I do, but instead of that, Walter Kennedy, you, and all the other big shots take money out of my pocket to put into yours. I want a better commission deal, and I want a company car. That's not too much to ask." With that Don stood up and leaned against the door in Jim's office, clearly waiting for a response.

Jim took a moment to think about what he had just heard. He wondered how his attempt to discipline Don for reprehensible behavior toward a co-worker had ended up being a compensation negotiation. Finally he responded, "This is why people find you so hard to work with, Don. You are always trying to avoid difficult issues by changing the subject and forcing your own agenda. Frankly, I am getting really sick of it."

"So does that mean I don't get any more money? How about a new car?" Don asked with a half smile on his face.

"Just get out of here and try to be nice," Jim said while turning away from Don and looking at an email that had just arrived on his computer.

Don, feeling confident that he had won that round, opened the door and walked out of Jim Balderson's office. "Don't forget to tell Walter Kennedy to cut me a better deal!" Don cracked as he walked down the hallway to his office.

Jim sat back in his chair wondering what his next move should be. "Should I fire him? Should I put an official letter of reprimand in his file? Should I make him apologize to Carol, or should I just let it go, like I have every other time?"

He didn't have the answer.

CHAPTER TWO
Meet Walter Kennedy

In business and in life a good reputation is the difference between success and failure...

CHAPTER 2

Meet Walter Kennedy

As he thought about Don, Jim's mind wandered to Walter Kennedy, who had hired him four years prior. He recalled how rigorous the hiring process was and how he wondered if he would ever be a member of the Joshua's Tires team.

Jim was working as a manager for another major tire firm in Vancouver when one of his old high school buddies gave him a call at home one night. His friend, Adam, was a Joshua's Tire Center manager in Calgary. He told Jim that Joshua's Tires was planning to open a new store in Vancouver and that he should apply. He explained that Joshua's usually promotes from within, but they had nobody available that could move there and because of the short time frame before opening day, they had no time to train a new manager. He explained to Jim that he had already recommended him to the CEO, Walter Kennedy, and that Walter would love to hear from him. Jim knew Joshua's from their reputation in the industry and knew that if he could become one of their managers, he would really have made it in the tire business. Jobs with Joshua's were hard to come by, and they were known to be picky about who they hired. They also had a reputation for being the fairest employer in the business with thousands of happy employees. Jim could hardly believe that his friend Adam had recommended him to Walter Kennedy, but he was very pleased that he did.

Jim called Walter in Toronto the next day and told him about his discussion with Adam.

"Well, I have to say that I am darned pleased to hear from you, Jim!" Walter said in a loud voice. "Adam tells me great things about you, and I am hoping that you are the answer to my prayers in Vancouver!"

"Well, I don't know about that, Mr. Kennedy, but I am very interested in coming to work for you!" Jim exclaimed.

"That sounds great, Jim, "Walter said. "But tell me why you are so interested in working for Joshua's?"

Without skipping a beat, Jim responded, "I have heard that you guys are the best. You have the best products, the best benefits program, the best incentive programs, and you have the fairest compensation package in the business. I have also heard that you have great training and mentoring programs. Adam told me that you consider each employee as a person, and you care about what happens to them at work *and* at home. That means a lot to me."

"All true," Walter responded with the sound of pride in his voice. "Our founder, Joshua O'Hare, worked very hard to make us the **employer of choice** in this industry, and it sounds like it is working. Well then, let's get you out to Toronto as soon as we can. I have never hired a manager without meeting him first. I want you to meet a couple of the other members of our team, and I want to put you through an aptitude profile process to see what makes you tick. Are you okay with all of that, Jim?"

Feeling like he had just won a lottery, Jim wasted no time in responding in the affirmative to Walter Kennedy, whom he considered a virtual legend in the tire business.

When he arrived in Toronto, a Joshua's employee in a familiar red Joshua's shirt was waiting in the arrival area of the airport and holding a sign up that read, "Jim Balderson for Joshua's Tire Centers." Jim thought this was a nice gesture and hoped it was also a sign of things to come. During the ride from the airport, the Joshua's employee, Karen, introduced herself to Jim and spoke eloquently and almost incessantly about Walter Kennedy and Joshua's Tires. She told Jim that she actually began her career at the firm working for the founder, Joshua O'Hare, in his first tire shop. She explained how Joshua had taken Walter under his wing when Walter was struggling in the insurance business. She expressed great admiration and respect for the work he had done since taking over from Joshua.

"I am a Joshua's girl, Jim, and I always will be. I can't even imagine working anywhere else, and I don't expect that I will ever have to worry about where my next meal is coming from. Joshua and Walter have looked after me very well," Karen said with pride.

Jim could feel the respect that Karen had for Walter and Joshua, but more than that, he could sense a much stronger emotion that could only be described as pure love. "This woman actually loves the place where she works and the people she works for," he thought to himself. "Wow, if everyone at Joshua's is like her, this has got to be a great place to work."

Joshua's Tire Centers had new headquarters. They had moved out of the cramped offices they had been using in their first tire shop and moved into the offices once occupied by the insurance company known as Shelton Saunderson Inc. Legend had it that they were the firm Walter Kennedy worked for before coming to Joshua's Tires. Jim had heard that they had been broken up and that the various branches had been sold off to the employees. Their head office was no longer needed, so when the lease was up, they closed it down. Because it was handy to Joshua's main store, Walter leased a portion of it for his burgeoning executive offices.

Before ushering Jim into Walter's office, Karen stopped and introduced him to Walter's assistant, Karla. They had a brief chat during which Karla mentioned that she had worked for Walter in the insurance business several years prior, and that when he asked her to leave Shelton Saunderson to work for him at Joshua's Tires, she didn't think twice about it and had never regretted it. "Let me give you one piece of advice, Jim," Karla said with a smile. "*Always remember: if it ain't fun, it ain't worth doing.*" She giggled after saying it, leaving Jim curious but somehow at peace.

Jim was also impressed by the fact that he had now met two Joshua's employees and both were totally dedicated and loyal to Walter Kennedy. "He's like a rock star," Jim thought.

Walter stood up from behind his desk when Karen and Jim came through the door. "There you go, Walter. I got him here in one piece!" Karen said with a laugh.

"I never doubted you for a minute, Karen," Walter said as Karen excused herself and left through Walter's open door.

Walter came around from behind his desk with his hand outstretched. The two men shook hands with a sense of urgency. "Great handshake, Jim," Walter said. "I like a firm but reasonable handshake. You know what I mean? I hate it when someone seems to be trying to break my fingers when we shake hands."

"I'm with you on that, Mr. Kennedy," Jim said nervously.

Sensing his discomfort, Walter softened his voice and said, "Call me Walter, Jim. Everyone does."

The two men talked for almost two hours. Walter led the conversation, but he did very little of the talking. Jim marveled afterward how Walter had an ability to ask questions in such a way that compelled him to offer up everything he could about himself. He also noticed that Walter seldom made a statement, but when he did it was always positive. At no time did he offer any negative commentary, nor did he respond to any negative commentary from Jim. He was in awe of Walter by the time the conversation was over. He had bared his soul, and now he assumed Walter would tell him if he had the job or not. He was about to find out that it wouldn't be quite that simple.

"You know something, Jim; I like you. However, I don't rely on just me anymore. I want you to meet a couple of folks who work very closely with me, and then we will sit you in front of a computer and put you through that aptitude profile I mentioned on the phone," Walter said with a smile.

As Jim followed Walter down the hallway of Joshua's head office he noticed that on every few feet of wall, there were pictures of groups of employees, individual employees, and employees in front of tire stores. "Not much artwork in here, but they sure do seem to like their employees," he thought. This was so unlike the head office of his current employer where you couldn't find a single picture of an employee, but which had a lot of expensive artwork that seemed somehow out of place in a tire company's headquarters.

Suddenly Walter stopped and then disappeared inside a room. "Come on in, Jim," he heard Walter say from inside the room.

As Jim entered the Joshua's boardroom he saw two people seated at the far end of the expansive oak table. "These two great folks are Bella and Joel, my managers of sales and operations. Bella does sales and Joel does ops. I want them to have a chat with you to see how they like you and to help me sort out exactly where you might fit in with our organization," Walter said with a smile before turning on his heel and exiting the room, closing the door behind him.

A second later the door opened again and Walter stuck his head in saying, "I hate closed doors, but this room is used for a lot of impromptu meetings and you three should have some privacy." With that, the door closed and Walter disappeared again.

Bella was a very professional appearing lady in her early forties. She had short brown hair and flawless, almost transparent white skin. She was dressed in a dark blue business suit and a white blouse that was buttoned to her neck. Despite her deliberate effort to dress conservatively, she could not hide her femininity. Jim found her quite attractive. Joel appeared to be in his early fifties. He had a beard and was graying a little in his chin area. He had a thick mop of curly hair that was nicely trimmed. He wore wire-rimmed glasses and tended to look through the bottoms of the lenses more than the tops, which indicated they were bifocals. He wore a black blazer with a white shirt, striped gray tie and gray flannel pants. In Jim's eyes, he looked like a businessman should look.

"These are not your typical tire shop employees," Jim thought to himself. They look like bankers. He suddenly realized that the tire business was much more than just the installation of tires on rims. It was very big business, and people who have to make multi-million dollar deals everyday need to look like they belong in a boardroom anywhere in the world.

"So tell us a little about yourself," Bella said enthusiastically. Joel, staring into Jim's eyes, said nothing.

Jim started out by telling them about his current job. He spoke freely about the size of his firm, their market share, how many employees report to him, and how he spends his day.

"That's all well and good, Jim. It sounds like you have the experience to work in one of our stores, but I would like to know a little about your personal life. I don't want to pry, but I do believe that the mental and emotional well being of our employees is governed to a large part by how well adjusted they are away from work. Do you mind talking about that?" Joel asked politely.

Jim was a little taken aback by this line of questioning, but he knew that Joel meant business and if he didn't answer, he might lose this opportunity. He spoke proudly about his wife, Wanda, his two sons and their mongrel dog, Sparky. Joel and Bella had a good laugh when he told them about how Sparky has a huge appetite for shoes, and how everyone in his family has to keep their footwear on an upper shelf so Sparky can't chew them up and bury the remains in the backyard.

The interview lasted almost exactly one hour, and at the end of it he shook hands with Bella and said goodbye to her as Joel directed him to a private office. Once inside the office Joel had him sit in front of the computer. He wrote down an access code and password and showed Jim how to begin using the program. When he was satisfied that Jim was ready to begin completing the survey, Joel left the room. He was given one hour to answer a number of multiple choice questions and word association quizzes. He wondered how any of the questions or the answers he was giving could possibly have any bearing on whether or not he should be hired.

When he was done, he left the office and wandered down the hall looking for Joel. He found him just a couple of offices away.

"All done, Jim?" Joel asked.

"Yes sir, I am," Jim responded triumphantly, before saying, "But, I can't even imagine how any of that stuff can tell you if I am right for the job or not."

"Ha ha," Joel laughed. "It is a mystery to everyone, but mark my words, that little survey you just completed will tell us quite accurately what kind of behavior we can expect from you and what motivates you. From that, we will have a better idea of how to deal with you and what kind of work you are best suited for."

"Well, Joel, I will have to trust you on that." Jim said skeptically. "When do I find out if I am the right guy for Joshua's?"

"Once we get the results back from the survey and have had a chance to look at them, Walter will have another meeting with you. Go back to your hotel, relax and enjoy the city. Be here at 2:00 PM tomorrow and I will review your aptitude profile with you, and then Walter will have his turn," Joel responded.

Jim, unable to contain his amazement, said, "Wow, a two-day interview. I have never heard of anything like it."

"Well, Jim, around here we believe that we need to spend a lot of time making sure that we are hiring the right folks for the right jobs so that we can avoid a lot of wasted time and unpleasantness months or years down the road. It worked for Joshua, and it is working for Walter, so we are all behind it," Joel explained.

"Gotcha, Joel. See you tomorrow afternoon," Jim said as he pushed the *L* button on the elevator. As he descended to the street, he wondered if the computerized survey would make or break him. He would not sleep well that night, but he knew that if accepted, he would be working for one of the best firms in the business. The anticipation was almost more than he could stand.

When Jim entered the office the next day, Joel was ready for him. "Come on in and let me tell you all about yourself," Joel laughed.

"I can hardly wait," Jim offered.

Joel explained that there are several parts to any aptitude profile. The basic elements that the employer wants to identify are behaviors and motivators. Some profiles can also determine cognitive ability and personality strengths and weaknesses.

"What this profile is telling me, Jim, is that you are motivated primarily by three things: money and the trappings of wealth, knowledge and learning, and to some extent, power. You like to be in charge and you like to control your environment and the people in it. Would you agree?"

"Uh huh," was all Jim could answer before Joel continued.

"Now, let's move to your behavior. The profile tells me that naturally you tend to be moderately dominant in most situations. You are not a shrinking violet, but you aren't Attila the Hun either. You are very optimistic and trusting of others, and you tend to believe that you can get whatever you want out of life with your charm. You think quickly, react quickly, and you will act on very little information. You are neutral to rules and regulations. You accept that we need rules in order to allow society and business to operate successfully, but you might try to find a way around the rules in order to achieve your goals." Joel stopped at this point to observe Jim's reaction and read his perceptions.

"My God, Joel! I can't believe you got all of that out of those questions I answered," Jim stated emphatically.

"Yes, it is pretty amazing stuff all right. Do you agree with it or not?" Joel asked.

"For the most part it is bang on. I think it might not be quite right in work situations though. I really don't trust everyone I deal with or work with, and I am not always optimistic," Jim challenged.

"Quite right!" Joel shot back. "I can see that in the report, too. You tend to adapt downward in that area, which suggests that in your current work environment you lack optimism and trust. That might help explain why you are here today applying for another job. Right?"

Jim was taken aback by Joel's question. No one at Joshua's Tire Center had asked him why he was willing to leave his current employer. No one had asked him how well he liked his current job. Now he knew why. It really didn't matter to them. This profile report told them everything they wanted to know about him. In their minds, whatever he had done in the past or was doing presently had no bearing on what he would do for them in the future. "Right, Joel," was all Jim answered.

"Okay, now we are going to move on to what we will see in you and how you feel about yourself," Joel announced. "I am seeing that you are quite self confident, have a great sense of self direction, and might be just a little bit arrogant from time to time." Joel stopped speaking and peered over his glasses at Jim, waiting for a comment.

"Arrogant?" Jim asked, not wanting an answer. "So this report says I am arrogant. Do you think I am arrogant, Joel? I don't think I am arrogant!"

"That one always gets them," Joel laughed. "The fact of the matter is that you are not currently displaying any indication of arrogance. What the report is telling me is that under circumstances where you are convinced that you are right, when you know in your heart that yours is the best course of action, you will drive forward with little regard for the opinions of others. You will have such great confidence in your own abilities that you will stop listening, and you will attempt to control the situation so that your point of view wins. At that moment in time, some people might feel that you are acting arrogantly. Does that make sense?"

"Okay, I get it. The report is telling you what might be expected. Not necessarily what goes on all the time," Jim offered.

"Yes, to some extent that is correct. It gives us an overview of *who* you are based on the myriad of elements that make up your personality. It gives us this information because of the way you answered the questions on the survey. Everything I am seeing here is what you provided, so it is in fact *you*. What the computer cannot do is read and understand stimulus that has not actually occurred yet. A traumatic, life-changing event in the future, for example, will have a significant effect on how you might answer the survey questions, and a very different report would result. For the most part, however, this report has provided us with an accurate image of who you are right now. It tells us how you will react in a relaxed natural setting and how you adapt to your environment under pressure or stress, such as when you are at work. If we use the report to its maximum benefit, it will allow us to work with you for the best utilization of your talents," Joel said confidently.

"Okay, it all makes sense, but I still don't think I am arrogant," Jim stated with a smile. Both men laughed.

Moving on, Joel pointed out that Jim generally had a fair amount of empathy toward others, was good with systems and had a natural understanding of how he could contribute to the success of the business. He had a good deal of common sense, and he was clearly comfortable in his current role. Joel also let Jim know that the profile report indicated that he had strong cognition in most areas and could be trained to handle almost any position. Jim learned that he was competitive and customer oriented, which did not come as a surprise to either man.

Joel put down the report and looked at Jim, saying, "Most importantly, Jim, you are very well balanced. What we see on the outside is very much in tune with what you feel on the inside. That is important to us because it means you will react appropriately in most situations."

Finally, Jim asked the question he had wanted to ask for two days, "So do I get the job?"

"I will let Walter fill you on that little matter," Joel said with a big smile. "What I will tell you is that this report tells me that with a little training and orientation, you could easily manage any one of our branches. You have all of the natural skills, talents, and attributes. Bella and I have both made our recommendation to Walter, but he likes to make the final decision on our managers, so let's go down to his office and see if we can get you in to see him."

The two men walked briskly down the hall toward Walter's office. They both carried themselves high and had a bounce in their steps. Joel liked Jim a lot and was happy to see such a bright young man joining the firm. Jim sensed that he was about to embark upon a new career and could barely contain his excitement.

When Karla saw them coming, she smiled and said, "Go right in guys. Walter is expecting you."

Again, when Walter saw them coming he stood up from behind his desk. This time he walked straight to Jim and embraced him. "Welcome aboard, buddy," was all he needed to say. Jim's heart was pounding so hard that he thought it would come right out of his chest.

Walter explained that Joel had debriefed him on the report earlier that day, and that if Joel and Bella were happy with Jim, he would be more than happy to hire him. "Having me bless the union is just a formality that I like to observe. It is important to me that you know that I want you here and that I am supporting you fully and completely. Do you have any questions for me?" Walter asked.

"When do I start work, Boss?" Jim asked with a huge smile.

"As soon as Joel gets the paperwork done, I guess," Walter said. "Now remember, I am the CEO, but I am not one of those guys who spends his time having expensive lunches and riding around in limos. I work here just like you, and I want to be kept abreast of anything significant that is going on. I will not micro-manage you, and I will respect that our Vancouver branch is your own personal show. However, I want you to keep in mind that I am here for you. Call me any time and I promise I will speak with you. If I am busy when you call, I will always call you back. We are in this together, Jim, and we all need to be part of the Joshua's team."

Jim never forgot Walter's final words that day.

CHAPTER THREE
Positive Reinforcement

*You must first seek to understand
the motivation before you can
fairly judge the behavior…*

CHAPTER 3

Positive Reinforcement

Jim's mind wandered back to the problem at hand. He simply could not allow Don to destroy the morale in his store. He had to find a way to either get him on board with the rest of the staff or get rid of him altogether. The second option was not at all appealing.

Jim had called Walter from time to time over the past four years, usually with news of positive developments or to ask for Walter's in-depth knowledge of sales matters or industry intelligence. This time he needed Walter's help with Don. He wondered what Walter would tell him.

"Hi, Jim. Great to hear from you! How is Vancouver these days?" Walter asked with a smile in his voice.

"Oh, things are fine here, Walter. I have one little problem that I need your help with, though. You know my salesman, Don?" Jim asked.

"Of course I do," Walter responded. "His dad works for me here in head office. Don started with us here in Toronto, and then after a two-year stint in Portland, we moved him up to Vancouver to help you out when your shop first opened. What kind of problem do you have with Don?"

Summoning up his all his courage, Jim responded, "Frankly, Walter, I am sick to death of his attitude, and I am considering termination."

"Wow, that's a drastic step, Jim! Tell me more," Walter said with concern.

Jim told Walter the story about Don's public admonishment of Carol. That shocked Walter, but he asked to hear more. Jim told him that Don had a generally bad attitude with everyone in the store, and he went on to explain that Don had an attitude of superiority and arrogance that manifested itself in rudeness and negativity. He would offer no praise or credit to anyone for good work they might do, and he routinely pounced on mistakes, pointing them out for all to hear. Walter was particularly concerned by the fact that Don was negative about Joshua's Tires and his management team.

Jim went on to explain that when Don is with his wife and kids, it is a completely different story. Around them he is quiet and polite. It is almost as if he is sheltering them from himself and protecting them from his true nature. He is also great with his clients. It is almost as if he is putting on a great *act* when he is dealing with them.

At that point Walter interjected, "You are partly right, Jim. Don is different in front of his family because he needs them, and he loves them dearly. They are his only source of constant security and he doesn't want to lose them. What you are seeing when he is with his family is perhaps the most genuine Don of all. Love is perhaps the strongest motivator that human beings have, and it surpasses all other feelings. His clients are the people who justify his existence and provide him with a feeling of belonging. He needs them too. So in fact, he *is* acting in order to maintain his relationships with them. He is giving the performance of a lifetime."

"So why is he such a monster with his co-workers, Walter? Why doesn't he put on a nice act for them? He really is bad news for all of us!" Jim complained.

"Jim, I am going to tell you some things about Don that you must keep completely confidential. Don's dad has filled me in on a few issues that will help explain where he is coming from. You must, however, promise that you won't discuss this with anyone because it might be hurtful to Don and his dad." Walter paused and waited for a positive response.

"I promise, Walter. Unfortunately, I need this guy so I am ready for anything you can tell me that will help," Jim said in anticipation.

Walter began again. "Don has ADHD, Jim. He knows he has it, and he knows that it affects his ability to focus and to function like everyone else. He won't take medication for it, and he avoids the subject whenever anyone in his family brings it up. Attention Deficit Hyperactive Disorder is more common than you might think, Jim. Some people think it is exclusive to kids, but a lot of adults have it. Some seek out treatment and others just live with it."

"Why does that make him such a monster to other people, Walter?" Jim asked.

"Well, I am not a doctor, Jim, but I suspect that his rudeness and arrogance are not symptoms of ADHD; they are cover ups for his condition. He attacks first before others can attack him. He was a troubled child because of his condition, you know. He ran away from home when he was fifteen, and his dad actually asked him to leave home when he was nineteen. His parents couldn't handle him, and they were desperate to make a normal life for their other children. They actually wanted him out of the way so they could focus on the other kids. Don would deliberately break things, argue over nothing, fight with his brothers and constantly insult and ridicule his younger sister. He was quick to anger but he seldom carried a grudge. He did poorly in school despite an incredible ability to memorize huge amounts of information and regurgitate it on command. He is actually very intelligent. Despite his potential to turn out good work in school, his teachers found him disruptive and unable to focus for any length of time. He spent a lot of time in the principal's office. After finishing high school, he wandered around the country from one job to the next until he found us." Walter paused to collect his thoughts.

Sensing the pause, Jim asked sarcastically, "So, can you fill me in on exactly why we hired this guy?"

Walter thought for a moment before answering, "I will take the responsibility for that decision, Jim. I have absolute respect and admiration for his dad, and frankly, I hoped we could rehabilitate Don and make him into a good citizen. When I hired him he was perfectly well behaved, and he got along well with almost everyone here in Toronto. He started out doing quite well after we sent him to Portland, but by the end of the second year when he became quite successful and very busy, he was beginning to make mistakes. He often forgot orders and blamed others for his negligence. He hadn't gotten to the point of being as obnoxious as you are describing, but he did spend a lot of time deflecting blame. I sent him to Vancouver to help you because he had become one of our top sales guys. I really didn't expect the behavior that you are seeing now.

I can tell you that when we profiled him, he tested out as being money-driven, highly dominant, and quite low on the social awareness scale. That would help to explain a lot of the difficulty you are experiencing. His major motivation is making money by whatever means he can. He is naturally pushy and quick to anger, and he is probably not even aware of the emotional harm he is doing to the people he is interacting with. I would bet that he doesn't even understand why his words are offensive."

"Well, I do have to say that he is a heck of a good salesman, but he does make a lot of mistakes and his behavior gets worse every day. I am probably going to start losing people because of him, and I can't afford that either. What do you think I should do now?" Jim asked politely yet almost desperately.

"That's a tough question, Jim," Walter stated matter-of-factly. "I guess you have to decide whether or not he is salvageable or if he is such a threat to your overall operation that you need to get rid of him."

Jim's mind wandered to an imaginary scene of him calling Don into his office and telling him that he is fired. He didn't like that picture, so he snapped out of it and began speaking again. "I guess I want to salvage him, Walter, but I really have no idea how to deal with him. Can you give me a clue?" Jim pleaded.

"Become his friend, Jim," Walter said. "He doesn't trust very many people because he is afraid they will let him down or discover his secret and use it against him. He only trusts people that are close to him like his wife and kids. If you want to control him, you need to get his respect, his trust, and ultimately his friendship. Once he trusts and respects you, he will want to please you, and then he will be receptive to your management needs. He will understand that when you are asking him to change his attitude and treat people better, it is something that is important to you, the company, and ultimately *himself*.

Don is kind to clients because he needs them. That is a completely different motivation. His condition doesn't affect his business sense. His clients will always enjoy doing business with him because he is great at evaluating the personalities of his clients and *acting* like them. He is brilliant at relationship building in small doses such as during client calls. Because he is heavily motivated by money, he has figured out how to make a lot of it for Joshua's and for himself. That's what makes him valuable.

The problem is that when he is in front of people for more than a few hours, as is the case with co-workers, he loses focus and actually wants to drive them away. Because of his hyperactivity, he says a lot of things without thinking them through. When he sees an opportunity to find fault with others, he takes advantage of it. Don has been *acting out* all of his life, and a lot of the bad attitude his co-workers are experiencing is a result of many years of conditioning, born of self-defense that started when he was child. He got in so much trouble in school and at home that it became natural for him to point the finger of blame at those around him. By doing that he hoped his own failings might be overlooked as the focus shifted to others. It also gave him the opportunity to feel superior during the time that the other person's mistakes were under the microscope. That helped his ego and fed his arrogance. Little has changed since he became an adult.

Don's effort to mask his disability is not totally uncommon, and it is often found in people with learning disabilities of various types. ADHD is only one of the many learning disabilities that afflict a fairly large percentage of our workforce. Interestingly, people with learning disabilities can become very successful. Their determination to overcome their disability often gives them the drive to be the best and the tenacity to keep fighting. Fortunately, they don't all end up with a negative attitude like Don."

"And strangely enough, despite his bad attitude, Don has a lot of friends. How do you explain that?" Jim asked.

"Yes, Don has a lot of friends, but he is only very close to a small number of them, Jim," Walter said. "Most of them are people he meets through his sales efforts. He is smart enough to know that a large network of influential people is the secret to success in sales. As much as some of his friends feel very close to him, he would think nothing of dropping them if he no longer had a use for them or if he couldn't get his way with them. Another segment of his social circle only socializes with him because they know he is successful and because he also knows a lot of influential people. They hang out with him to further their careers, and many of them would also drop him if he no longer fulfilled their need to enhance their sphere of influence.

Your challenge is not to have just another business-based relationship, but rather to be his soul mate, someone he can rely on and go to in times of need. You must become his brother, his father, his minister and his coach. You need to be the first person he thinks of when he is in trouble. He needs to know that you respect his accomplishments, and he needs to feel that his disability, although very real, is invisible to you. Praise him when he does well and let him know that you care about what he does. He will respect you if he feels you are there for him unconditionally. You must also exercise patience when he lets you down. He will fall back on his old ways from time to time, and if you lose your temper, you will also lose all of the progress you have made. Open up to him and tell him directly and honestly how you feel. The more vulnerable you are to him, the more he will trust you, and ultimately the more he will like you. Be his best friend, Jim, and you will be able to control him because he will do anything for you. The bottom line is that you must always think positive. I want you to have **positive passion** in your dealings with Don and all of your employees."

"Wow, Walter. That's a tall order," Jim said with a sigh. "He is so nasty that I just feel like hauling him into my office and reading him the riot act."

"You won't change him with discipline or threats. Don knows he is a great salesman and he knows that our competitors would snap him up in a New York minute if we let them. If you push him too hard, he will be working against you in no time. It's your show, Jim, but I think you need to try to get him on your side. If, on the other hand, you feel you have tried everything and he is simply a lost cause, then fire him quickly before he does any more damage. The challenge you have is that if you keep him and he doesn't change, he might do irreparable damage to the morale in your store and end up working for the competition anyway. On the other hand, if you can *fix* him, he will make your store even more successful than it is now, and he might just become a long-term ally. I'm sure glad it's your decision and not mine," Walter said with a laugh.

"Thanks a lot," Jim said sarcastically.

"Hey, Jim, I told you when I hired you that I was here to help you, but that I would *not* micro-manage you. What we have here is a pretty good example of that. I guess I could just fly out there and have a chat with Don myself and ask him to shape up. However, that would only work in the short term. I think he respects me enough to fall into line for a while, but only someone who works with him everyday can keep him on the straight and narrow. That person is you, Jim. Are you up to it?" Walter asked.

Sensing that Walter was annoyed with him, Jim said confidently, "Absolutely, Walter. Please don't let my lack of enthusiasm shake your confidence in me. I have been battling with this guy for so long that I am a little despondent. However, I know that you are right, and now I have to take the bull by the horns and win him over. Thanks for everything, Walter. I hope I don't let you down."

"Keep a stiff upper lip, Jim. I know that guys like Don can be a real handful. Please understand that I know you are doing your best and that I will support you no matter what. You *are* my guy in Vancouver, and you're doing a great job. Without you, we would have nothing out there," Walter said in a kindly tone.

"Thanks, Walter. That means a lot to me," Jim said sincerely.

With that, the call ended. Walter had learned from his mentor, Joshua O'Hare, several years prior that every call should end on a high note. No one in his organization should ever feel worse at the end of a call than they did when the call started. No one should ever be left with the feeling that the person they report to disrespects them or doesn't fully support them. Walter knew that through positive reinforcement, *anything* is possible. That is what made Joshua's Tire Centers strong when Joshua was running it, and that is what made it even more successful under Walter's direction. Walter believed that if he had to the make the choice of having only one business principle to work with, ***positive passion*** would be the one he chose.

Walter also knew that the same principle would work for Jim in his dealings with Don.

* * *

Within only a few months, Don became a model employee. He and Jim became friends and close allies at work. Jim not only opened up to Don, but he created some positive energy in him. Jim challenged Don to fix some of the problems he saw around the store rather than just complaining about them. When Don agreed to help, Jim gave him the title Sales Manager so he would have the authority to effect change. Armed with the authority and responsibility to make a difference, Don performed some very special magic, imparting his natural sales skills to everyone else in the store. The entire staff rallied around him, and their sales numbers went through the roof.

When they weren't making their store the best performing tire shop in the region, the two men spent a lot of time fishing and golfing together. Jim knew he had won Don over on the day Sparky chewed up one of his shoes and buried it in the back yard. Don just laughed and said, "I guess that makes me a member of your family, eh, Jim?"

Jim finally understood Walter's secret of ***positive passion*** that day, and he knew he would never forget the power of it.

Don would go on to become one of the best performing sales managers that Joshua's ever had. Walter knew that as long as Jim Balderson was there for him, Don would be devoted to his job and always give his best.

CHAPTER FOUR
That's Not My Job!

There is no job too big or too small. At the end of the day, the only job that matters is the one that got done...

CHAPTER 4

That's Not My Job!

Walter had a pet peeve for the expression, "That's not my job." Whenever he heard someone saying it, he called them into his office and explained to them that saying, "That's not my job," gave the impression that the jobs at Joshua's Tires were so specific and so complex that employees could not help each other or cover for each other in times of illness or when things were very busy. It also seemed to imply that only certain people could help clients with their needs. To Walter, every employee was a salesperson for Joshua's Tires, and every employee had an obligation to help everyone else whenever possible.

Of course, Walter acknowledged that there are jobs requiring a high degree of technical skill or formal training that simply cannot be done by just anyone. In most cases common sense would dictate that people who are not capable or qualified to do something would not be asked to do those things. Walter's ire had often been raised when he heard an employee being rebuked by another when asking for help with a common or obviously easy task. He became even angrier when an employee refused to assist a customer when there was no apparent good reason not to do so.

He knew instinctively, for example, that when an employee in the tire sales department refused to show a client where to park his car when asked by a busy service coordinator, there was a much deeper issue. When a busy receptionist was rebuked when she asked a parts person to cover the phone because she was called away to attend to an emergency with her baby, Walter knew he had a problem. When an accounting person refused to discuss an incorrect invoice with a customer because she was not in the receivables department, and when a sales person refused to help a mechanic by moving a customer's car out of the way of the service bay door, his blood boiled.

Walter knew that customer service suffered whenever his employees began to feel their jobs were more important than everyone else's or when they became so difficult they would refuse to do anything except what they felt their jobs entailed. These employees are more than just stubborn. They are, in fact, disengaged. When they get to the point of saying, "That's not my job," they have in fact become toxic and must be dealt with before they begin dragging other employees into their web of disengagement.

It is common for people who are in the wrong job or who are uncomfortable and unhappy at work to say, "That's not my job." The problem is not with what they are being asked to do, but simply that they hate the job they have and would prefer to do *nothing* to assist their co-workers or to improve the fortunes of their employer. As much as everyone knows that happy, helpful people who are always ready to roll up their sleeves to assist another employee are the most popular and upwardly mobile people in any firm, we still find disengaged people who are willing to risk their jobs, their careers and their very futures in order to maintain their right to say, "That's not my job."

Jane Meadows gave a lot of thought to whether or not she should call Walter Kennedy about a serious problem that was brewing in her Winnipeg tire shop. Her accounting clerk, Erica Robertson, was causing untold grief in her store. Not only did she refuse to assist anyone with virtually anything, but she had recently begun encouraging other employees to refuse to do anything that did not fall specifically into their job descriptions. Jane knew these things were going on because she had been given reports from three different employees during annual performance reviews.

Jane knew Walter Kennedy only slightly, and from what she knew of him, he was a hands-on CEO who knew what was going on in almost every branch in the country. The numbers in her shop were good, but because of the creeping cancer of employee disengagement, customer service was beginning to suffer, and she knew it was just a matter of time before her numbers started to slump. She had tried to speak to her negative employee, but when confronted, Erica simply stated that she was doing nothing wrong and denied that she had encouraged anyone in the branch to refuse to do anything outside their job description. Erica's performance was adequate, and the duties that fell specifically within her area of responsibility were always completed accurately and on time. Jane had no grounds for dismissal and simply did not know what to do.

The final straw for Jane came when she overheard Erica telling one of her sales clerks that she shouldn't come in early anymore because her example was setting a precedent that no one else wanted to live up to. Jane was standing behind a rack of brake parts where she could not be seen, and when she heard the first few words, she decided to do a little spying on her least favorite employee. When the clerk protested, Erica said, "Look here, Ashley, just do your job and nothing more. There is no glory in doing extra work around here, and if you keep it up, the rest of us will make your life very unpleasant indeed!"

Ashley was a very loyal employee who worked long hours because she liked her job, not because she had to. She was always looking for ways to help others. From a management perspective, she was a model employee. Through the eyes of a disengaged employee, however, she was a threat who must be stopped.

Jane was so shocked by what she heard that she made a hasty retreat to her office without saying anything to anybody. She knew then that she was in over her head and needed some help. She picked up the phone on her desk and dialed Walter Kennedy's direct line.

"Well, hello there, Jane!" Walter said cheerily after Jane had introduced herself. "It seems to me that I haven't actually spoken with you since our last managers' conference in Chicago last year. To what do I owe this honor?"

"I am sorry to have been so non-communicative, Walter, but I have been very busy with some serious issues out here, and I need to pick your brain. Do you have time to speak with me?" Jane asked with a serious tone in her voice.

"All the time in the world, Jane," Walter said confidently. He sensed that something was seriously wrong and knew he had to hear more. "So tell me Jane, what's bothering you, and how can I help?"

"Well, Walter, I have a really negative staff member in my accounting department named Erica who seems hell-bent on destroying our operation. She is constantly causing problems and is determined that neither she nor anyone else should ever do anything more than they have to. I have had reports from other staff members about her coaching them on how to reduce the amount of work they do in a day, how to *appear* busy, how to make sure the company doesn't take unfair advantage of them, and to make sure no one does anything to help the managers. She also tells them that they should be sure to always take all of their holidays, personal days, sick days and any other days they can get away with."

Jane then told Walter about Erica's discussion with Ashley before saying, "I have talked to her and she denies everything. Frankly, Walter I am out of ideas. I just don't know what to do."

Walter could hear the strain in Jane's voice and knew she was on the verge of tears. He knew instinctively that Erica was a member of the infamous *that's-not-my-job squad*, the people he dreaded the most. He decided to be very direct with Jane, immediately saying, "Jane, you have a problem employee, and you have to deal with her now before she can do any more damage. This is the kind of person who can destroy the morale in your shop before you get out of bed in the morning. You have to deal with her now before she has an opportunity to inject all of your employees with her toxic venom."

Jane was taken aback. She did not know Walter very well, and she had always heard that he believed in a business theory everyone called **positive passion**. Although she knew Erica was a huge negative force in her operation, she was surprised that Walter had become so negative so soon into their conversation. Jane wanted to speak but could not summon up the words to complete her thoughts.

Sensing her discomfort, and almost as if he had read her mind, Walter spoke again. "Look, Jane, I know it is in our job descriptions as managers to take the high road and think positively and optimistically at all times. In fact, I preach that concept in the seminars I run. However, this phenomenon of *that's not my job* is one that has to be treated very seriously. The most positive thing we can do for ourselves and for our employees is to eliminate it at all costs.

What you are hearing from Erica is the ranting of a person who, for some reason or other, is extremely unhappy in her job and perhaps in every facet of her life. She may be in the wrong job, or she may simply feel that the world is out to get her and that our company is just another example of society treating her unfairly. To people like her, the ideas of enjoying your day at work or doing more than you have to in order to improve the workplace are simply foreign concepts that may not be allowed to fester in her brain. She is probably so totally convinced of her negative view of life that she is determined to make certain everyone else feels the same way." With that, Walter stopped speaking in order to allow Jane a chance to respond.

"My goodness, Walter, I have to say that you seem to have nailed Erica and the attitude she is displaying around the store, but I still don't know what to do. I really don't know how to get through to her. Are you suggesting that I should just get it over with and fire her?"

"I am not suggesting anything, Jane. What I am saying is that you have to deal with her quickly and severely in order to protect yourself, your employees, and our store."

"Can you give me a hint, Walter? I simply don't know how to deal with her," Jane said in a defeated tone.

"Firstly, Jane, I need to know something from you. Is Erica a good worker and does she add value to your operation?" Walter asked.

"Oh, yes. When Erica puts her mind to her work, she is a real dynamo. She can pump out more work than almost anyone in the place when she is not focused on being negative," Jane answered quickly.

"Alright then, we have a place to start, and we have an employee we need to save. Open, honest communication is the only way to go with Erica, Jane. I don't know what you have said so far, but you need to challenge her on her threat to Ashley, and you need to tell her that her negative behavior will no longer be tolerated. You will have to write her up and put a copy of the letter of admonishment in her personnel file. Make sure you also send a copy to our head office Human Resources department. There are potential future legal implications here, Jane. We have to be certain that we have covered ourselves with appropriate warnings in the event that we have to terminate her in the future. I know it seems a bit harsh, but it must be done," Walter finished with a sigh.

"So what then, Walter?" Jane asked pleadingly.

"Then you begin to work with her. I don't know Erica, and I don't know what is on her mind. However, there may be something going on in her life that you can help her with. Perhaps you can turn her around. Once you are done with the warning discussion, bring your tone down a bit and ask her if you can help her. Ask her to open up to you. Point out to her that her attitude is different from everyone else's in the shop and that other employees have spoken with you about her. The idea here is that she probably hasn't accepted that she is doing anything wrong, and it is possible that she feels everyone else in the operation feels the same way she does. Give her some tough love, Jane. Let her know that you are on her side and want to help, but that you cannot tolerate her attitude any longer or allow her to contaminate the morale in the office."

"Okay. Thanks, Walter." Jane said with a quiet sigh.

"Don't worry, Jane," Walter said encouragingly. "If you treat Erica with respect while letting her know that you mean business, you will probably win her over. Always remain positive. Even your comments regarding her negative attitude should be made in a positive way. Make sure you use relaxed, inviting body language. Don't fall into the trap of losing your patience or your temper. If that happens, you will lose her respect and she will want to fight back. Speak with confidence but do not talk down to her. After every thought, confirm that she understands what you have said so you can confidently move on to the next subject. Never make unfounded accusations based on rumors and don't use terms like, "You always do this and you never do that. Hyperbole like that will only inflame the situation and allow an opportunity for another argument."

"Thanks, Walter. I think I can take it from here," Jane said with more confidence than she had exhibited since she first picked up the phone. "I will give it my best try."

"That's great, Jane. Let me know how it works out," Walter said in a kindly tone before hanging up the phone.

* * *

The following week, after Jane had given a lot of thought to what she had to do, she called Erica into her office. She walked up to Erica's desk and said in a very pleasant tone, "Erica, can I see you in my office right away, please?"

Erica sensed from Jane's body language and mannerisms that there was something very serious on Jane's mind. Her first reaction was defensive. "Am I in trouble, Jane? Have I done something wrong?" she asked, while desperately avoiding eye contact with Jane.

"Let's just go into my office and talk," Jane said softly.

When the two women entered Jane's office, Jane closed the door behind them. Erica remained standing until Jane walked behind her desk and sat down. Still standing, Erica asked in curt tone, "Should I sit or is this going to be short and sweet?"

"Oh, no, please sit down and relax, Erica," Jane said while looking into Erica's eyes with a smile. Jane knew that Erica was spoiling for a fight and that she had to remain calm and not fall victim to her natural urge to fight back.

"So why am I here?" Erica asked.

Jane thought for a moment before she spoke. "Well, firstly, Erica, I want you to know that I have always been impressed with your work. When you apply yourself, you are one of our best people. I have always admired the way you can focus on a job and get it done in record time with virtually no errors."

Erica relaxed, assuming this was going to be a much better meeting than she had been expecting. She decided to say nothing, choosing to wait for further compliments. She would soon be disappointed.

Jane began again, "Erica, I have to tell you that some of the behavior that you have been exhibiting here lately has been quite disturbing."

Erica squirmed uncomfortably in her chair. "What do you mean?" she asked defiantly.

"Well, frankly, I have had numerous reports of your advising some of our staff not to do any more work than they have to. You have complained that the management here doesn't care about our employees, and most importantly, I overheard you threatening Ashley," Jane said softly but with conviction.

At that point Erica sat back in her chair and almost shouted, "I never threatened her. What has she been telling you?"

"Erica, she hasn't told me anything," Jane said calmly. "Actually, she has never said anything negative about you at all. The fact of the matter is that I heard you telling her that if she kept coming in early, you were going to make her life very unpleasant. Why would you say such a thing?"

Knowing that she had been caught, Erica sat back in her chair with a look of defeat on her face. She spoke much more quietly this time. "Well, we all know that she is one of your favorites, and it just seems like she is doing everything she can to make the rest of us look bad. I don't like people who work so hard at being the *teacher's pet*."

"Firstly, she is not my favorite. I don't have a favorite. Secondly, when you talk about Ashley or anyone else, please don't lump the rest of our staff into your negative point of view. When you said that you *all* know she is my favorite, and that she is doing things to make the *rest* of you look bad, you were transferring your own personal fears to everyone else. Erica, you are the only one who feels that way. I have spoken to the rest of the staff, and they all like Ashley. She does not threaten them and they don't resent her. It is only you who feels that way." With that, Jane stopped speaking and sat back in her chair, staring into Erica's eyes.

"Oh, really. So I suppose you think I am just a terrible person," Erica said as tears began to well up in here eyes.

"Not at all, Erica," Jane answered. "You are a great worker and a valuable member of the staff. I just want to get to the bottom of this so I can help you be happy here."

Sensing that Jane was being genuine, Erica felt a renewed sense of encouragement and sat up straight in her chair, wiping the tears away. Her voice cracked as she asked, "So what are you going to do?"

Jane knew that she had Erica's attention now and that she must be very clear with her intentions and how she presented them. She spoke strongly and with determination, "Erica, your comments to Ashley can be considered harassment and are grounds for termination."

"Oh, no!" Erica gasped as tears began to flow from her eyes.

"Don't worry, Erica. I am not going to fire you this time," Jane said. "I will have to write a letter of warning to you, and it will form a permanent part of your record with us. If this kind of behavior continues, however, I will have no choice but to terminate you in the future. I am sure you can understand my position in this, can't you?"

"I suppose so, Jane. I just don't get why a simple disagreement between two employees is such a big deal for you," Erica said, still weeping.

Jane knew she had to lay her cards on the table now. "Erica, please understand this once and for all. You have no right to threaten anyone. Nor do you have any right to suggest to employees that they do less work than they are capable of. You act as if the people who provide your paycheck and the managers here are nothing but a bunch of tyrants. You drag everyone down with your negativity, and this attitude of, "That's not my job," is starting to affect our bottom line. I am here to tell you there is no job in this place that is below me, below you, or below anyone else on our payroll. I also want to make it clear that people like Ashley who will go the extra mile are not threats. They are model employees who will go much further in life and with this company than those who want to hold back and spend more time complaining than working."

Erica was in shock now. She knew that Jane meant business and that she had to make amends. "What can I do to make you happy?" she asked pleadingly.

"It's not about me, Erica. I am already happy. It would make better sense for me to ask how I can make you happy. You have really taken on a different persona lately, and frankly, I am worried about you. Is everything all right at home?" Jane asked.

"Yes, things are fine at home. Actually, I can hardly wait to get home every night. It is the only place where I am really happy."

"So what is making you unhappy at work then?" Jane questioned.

Erica did not really know how to answer the question. She knew that she hated coming to work in the morning and that she didn't enjoy her time while she was at work. Beyond that, she was unsure of what might be wrong. She had been unhappy for so long that it had become natural to her, and until today she had assumed that everyone else felt the same way. People who were happy at work annoyed her, and she was determined to make them unhappy as well. As she began to visualize and accept her own reality, she became acutely depressed. She began to weep again before saying, "I don't know, Jane. I am just miserable all the time." With that she began to sob uncontrollably.

"Please don't cry, Erica," Jane asked politely. "We can work through this together. I think the first thing we need to do is find out what's bothering you. Tell me something; do you like the work you do?"

"Oh, yes. I love accounting. I have always liked doing the books, and I love putting together spreadsheets and flow charts. When you hired me, I thought I had found my dream job," Erica said enthusiastically.

Jane was becoming perplexed. She had discovered that Erica had a good home life and loved her job, yet she was miserable at work. She hadn't gotten anywhere. She knew she had to forge on. "Do you think your workload is fair, Erica?" she asked.

"Well, actually I have talked to some of the accounting clerks in some of the other branches, and I know that my workload is much larger. They have assistants to help them with a lot of things that I do myself, and on average, they have fewer transactions to deal with each month. I can keep up, but if you want to know the truth, my job is much tougher than anyone else's in the same position," Erica stated matter-of-factly.

Jane knew she was getting somewhere now. "So why have you not mentioned this to me before?" she asked.

Erica squirmed a bit and took a deep breath before saying, "Frankly, I assumed you must know how much work I have to do. You are the boss after all. Besides I always felt that you didn't like me and were loading me up just to make me miserable."

Jane was stunned by this response. "Why do you think I don't like you? I don't recall ever doing anything to make you feel that way. Wow, Erica that really comes as a surprise to me. I like you as well as I like anyone who works here."

"If you like me so much, then why don't you include me in anything?" Erica asked seriously.

"What do you mean, Erica?" Jane asked.

"Well, whenever there is a staff meeting to discuss the direction of the store, you listen to everyone but me. If I try to offer anything, you shut me down by making it clear that the accounting department doesn't know anything about running a business. We are just here to count the moncy. Then last year when you took some of the staff to a conference in Toronto, not only did you not take me, you took two people that have far less seniority than me. And I would really like to go to one of those golf tournaments that you take the sales people to. Let's face it, Jane, there are not many incentives for accounting people in this place. Or maybe you just don't like me!" Erica exclaimed.

Jane sat back in her chair with a blank look on her face. She needed to take some time to process what she had just heard. Now she knew why Erica had become a toxic employee and why she wanted to make sure that no one else in the store could be happy either. She was a person of high self-esteem who believed that she had more to offer than simply doing an accounting clerk's job. Each time she was excluded from company events and corporate planning sessions, her self-image suffered. Her reaction to having her ego bruised was to strike back by working behind the scenes to harm the very place she worked. Jane knew instinctively that it was imperative she repair the harm that had been done as soon as possible.

Jane began to speak in earnest, "Erica, all I can say is, I am sorry. You are quite right in everything you have said. I guess I have taken you for granted. I see now that you have much more to offer this company than we have allowed, and I simply have not been listening to you. Let's change that right now. I am going to a regional management conference in Toronto next week, and I could sure use the help of a sharp accountant to help me with the budget session they have planned. Of course, you would have to endure a whole day of golf and a few dinners in top-notch restaurants, but I think you are up to it. What do you say? It could be fun," She said with a wink.

"Oh my gosh, Jane. I would love to go!" Erica exclaimed.

"Okay, it's a deal then. We leave next Tuesday, and we will be home on Friday just in time for you to spend the weekend with your family," Jane said with a smile.

Erica was so overcome with emotion that she began to shed tears of joy. Jane stood up, came around from behind her desk, and embraced her new ally.

* * *

When Walter Kennedy spied Jane at the opening night reception at the management conference, he made his way across the room to greet her. "Hi, Jane, great to see you again," he said.

"Hi Walter, please let me introduce you to my number one accounting clerk, Erica Robertson," Jane said with pride.

"Well, it *is* great to meet you," Walter said with a smile. Then he turned to Jane and gave her a wink and a nod that Jane knew indicated that he understood everything had turned out as they had hoped.

When Jane and Walter managed to find a quiet moment alone, she filled him in on her meeting with Erica. She could not say enough about how much she had learned about Erica and herself during their discussion. **Positive passion** had won out again, and Walter could not have been more proud of both Jane and Erica.

Later that evening at the dinner Walter was hosting for the conference delegates, he asked Jane to pass him the salt.

"Hey, that's not my job!" Jane yelled back.

Everyone at the table, including Walter, laughed uproariously.

Erica knew then that fun and laughter were welcomed at Joshua's Tire Centers. She was thrilled to be part of it, and she went on to become a happy and fully engaged employee who was admired by everyone in her store.

CHAPTER FIVE

Bosses Make Mistakes, Too

*The tragedy is not in being wrong.
The tragedy is in not listening to
those who might be right…*

CHAPTER 5

Bosses Make Mistakes, Too

Robert Wrigley knew he had to make the call. He really didn't want to talk to Walter Kennedy today, but he knew that if he didn't bring him into the loop now, there could be trouble later. Robbie, as his friends called him, knew that Walter was a hands-on kind of guy who would go to bat for anyone who asked for help. He also knew that Walter did not like failure, and as kind as he was, he would not stand for secrecy or deceit from his managers when it came to problems that could have negative effects on the finances of the company.

Robbie Wrigley was the Vice President of Sales for the southern Alberta region of Joshua's Tire Centers. The regional head office was in Calgary, and Robbie made his home there. He was an Alberta boy and had been in the tire business ever since he left high school. When he finished school in his home town of Lexington, Alberta, he immediately got a job at the local Joshua's Tire Shop. He started at the bottom, fixing flats and moving cars in and out of the shop. In a couple years he had moved into the mechanical side of the business, doing brake and muffler repairs. Although Robbie had a flair for working on cars, he had a burning desire to move into management. Every time Walter

Kennedy or one of his vice presidents dropped by to visit the branch manager, Robbie would hang around the office hoping to get an opportunity to be noticed and acknowledged. Robbie's manager, Bill Johnson, liked Robbie, and finally one day he took the opportunity to introduce him to Walter during one of his visits. Walter was as warm and charming as Robbie had heard him to be, and he was totally impressed. At that moment Robbie decided that he would be one of Walter's vice presidents some day.

Robbie's shot at management finally came a year later when the manager of a branch in the nearby town of Sackville sadly passed away. This was a very small town and the shop only had a staff of five, so there was absolutely no one available to take over. Always wanting to promote from within, Walter put out a call to all the branch managers in the region to recommend someone who could move to Sackville and manage the shop. Time was of the essence because the deceased manager had been very independent-minded and had never trained any of his employees to do the books, order the parts, pay the bills or do virtually anything other than work on the cars. They were floundering without him, and if help didn't come soon, the shop would fail.

Bill Johnson had always enjoyed Robbie's desire for management knowledge and had trained him on all aspects of purchasing, parts handling, computerized accounting and general record keeping. He hoped that Robbie would replace him some day, but he also knew that the smaller Sackville shop was the perfect place for his young protégé to hone his newly acquired management skills. He picked up the phone and called Walter as soon as he read Walter's email regarding the job opening.

"As much as I hate to say it, Walter, I believe I have your manager right here in Lexington," he said calmly.

"Wow, that's great Bill. Who do you have in mind and why on earth do you hate to say it?" Walter asked.

"You remember that kid, Robbie, I introduced you to about a year ago?"

"I sure do, Bill. I liked him a lot. He seemed really keen, and I took him for a heck of a nice young man."

"Well, you got that right, Walt. He is a little cocky, but he has a good heart. You know that I am planning to retire in a couple of years, and I have been training young Robbie to take over. Right now I think he probably already knows more about running this shop than I do. You know how these young guys take to computers and the like. Anyway, I was actually going to put his name forward to you when I saw you at the management conference in Calgary this October, but since this Sackville deal has come up, I think it would be unfair both to Robbie and to you to hold him back," Bill said with determination in his voice.

"That is what I have always admired about you, Bill. You always put the company first. If I could clone a bunch of guys like you, I would never have to worry again. Josh always said that about you too, you know. He thought the world of you," Walter said genuinely.

"Well you know, Walter, you have been pretty darned good to me, but Joshua was the *man*. I would have crawled across broken glass in a firestorm for that guy. He gave me a chance when I needed it most, and I would never knowingly let his company down. No offense meant, Walt, but I think you know where I am coming from," Bill said politely.

"No offense taken, Bill. I recall that Josh bought your business from you when you were having some financial woes. He didn't have to do it, but he saw something he liked in you. By the way, we have made good money from your shop ever since, so believe me when I tell you that Josh has always been happy with his decision, and so have I," Walter responded respectfully.

"Right on, Walt!" Bill said with a slight tone of impatience. Walter could tell that Bill was becoming uncomfortable with the discussion and wanted to move on, so he reverted back to the original conversation.

"I tell you what, Bill, I trust your judgment on this one, and we have an urgent need, so go ahead and tell the young man that he has the job. I will come out there next week and make it official. Tell him to start packing. Oh, and by the way, Bill, I owe you for this. When retirement time comes, talk to me personally and I will make sure you are well looked after," Walter offered.

"I will hold you to that, Walt. The kid is as good as gone. If he lets us down, I will personally drive over to Sackville and put a hurtin' on him. Ha, ha, ha!" Bill laughed deeply from his bulbous belly. Both men were still laughing when they hung up their phones.

What neither man knew about Robbie was the way he felt about himself. Because Walter did not take the time to administer an aptitude profile test on his newest manager, he did not have an opportunity to find out what was lurking beneath the surface of his psyche. There were two Robbies: the one that everyone could see and the one that existed invisibly inside his mind and his heart. The *internal* Robbie was imprisoned, waiting for a chance to get out.

Robert Wrigley was born in Lexington, Alberta, to Bonnie Dickinson. He never knew his father. Bonnie had left her abusive husband in Ontario when she learned she was pregnant with Robbie. She was so desperate to get away that she traveled all the way across the country to Alberta in search of a better life for her two year old son, Julian, and baby Robbie who she was still carrying. With two infant children and no real skills other than a knowledge and love of cows she had learned from her father on his farm in Northern Ontario, she felt that Alberta might be the place where she could finally settle down and live a good life. She was right. Shortly after Robbie was born in Lexington, she met a divorced rancher by the name of Jake Wrigley when she applied for a job as a bookkeeper at his successful cattle ranch. Jake liked Bonnie and was sympathetic to her situation as an unmarried mother with two infant children. In what seemed like no time, Jake fell in love with Bonnie and asked for her hand in marriage.

Jake was a great husband to Bonnie, but he treated Robbie and Julian as if they were not part of his family at all. Having had no children of his own from his first marriage, he thought he might enjoy the dynamics of being dad to a couple of little kids. Bonnie could not have been more happy, and the family appeared to be as solid and devoted as any other. However, the truth was that Jake was not able to embrace the idea of having two children who were not his own in his life, and he became more resentful of them with each passing day. He felt the kids were a wedge between him and his love for Bonnie. He was envious of the attention they received from her and the obvious love she had for them. In order to punish the boys for being there, without actually harming them, he worked them mercilessly hard on the ranch.

They were given so many chores that even grown men would have had trouble completing the work they were forced to do each day. When the work was done, there was never a "thanks" or a "job well done" from Jake. Usually he inspected their work and found fault with it. When he was in a particularly foul mood, he would make them start again and completely redo everything. Julian and Robbie complained to their mother, but she did nothing. Jake treated her well and provided for her every need, so she was not about to create a rift that might destroy her lifestyle. Besides, she was not fully aware of the extent of Jake's torment to her boys, and she knew it was common for children to exaggerate and complain about hard work.

Julian had a stoic sense of resolve, and he carried on being Jake's whipping boy without complaint until he graduated from high school. Robbie, on the other hand, grew more and more restless, and the need to escape from the only home he had ever known overwhelmed him. He was constantly in trouble with the teachers in his school, and he got into a lot of fights with classmates. When he was fifteen years old, Robbie could no longer stand it and ran away from home. He looked a lot older than his years due to long days in the sun working the fields. His complexion was dry and brown, and the muscles in his chest and arms were as toned and powerful as those of any grown man. Thanks to that and the fact that he lied about his age, he was able to land a job as a laborer with a pipeline crew. He spent the next four months away from the Wrigley home traveling all over Alberta installing oil and gas pipe, while learning how to smoke, drink, and speak a lot of foul language that he would never have heard at home. He also learned a lot about life and working with other men. He was truly enjoying his work and his new found freedom until one day when the foreman of the crew called him into the office trailer that had been set up in a gravel pit near the pipeline excavation.

"Robbie, git your butt in here right now!" The foreman yelled across the yard at him.

"What's up, Smokey?" Robbie hollered back.

"Never mind, just git in here and git in here now!" Smokey yelled in an exasperated tone.

As Robbie jogged across the yard, he noticed a very familiar pickup truck parked next to the office trailer.

"Darn!" he thought. "The old man finally caught up with me."

When Robbie stepped inside the trailer, Jake Wrigley and Smokey were waiting for him. Jake said nothing, allowing Smokey to take the lead.

"Young man, your dad here tells me that you are only fifteen years old and that you are a runaway," Smokey stated matter-of-factly. Robbie said nothing, but the look on his face spoke a thousand words. "I have to tell you, Robbie, that you are one of the best workers I have had on my crew in a very long time. I am going to be sorry to see you go, but I am afraid I have no choice but to send you packing with Jake here. When you get another few years under your belt, if you still feel like being a pipeline worker, give me a call and I will darned sure have a job for you, buddy."

Without speaking a word, Jake motioned to Robbie to leave the trailer. As Robbie and Jake walked across the yard and got into the pickup truck, Smokey said to himself, "Poor Robbie. His dad must be a real monster to chase a great kid like that out of his house."

As Robbie stepped onto the running board of Jake's big pickup truck, he feared he was about to bear the brunt of some things that he would not like. He did not know what Jake's response to his disappearance would be, but he assumed it would be less than pleasant. He was all too correct.

Jake said nothing until they were about ten miles from his ranch. As they turned down the gravel road that led to the house, he said, "You have really stepped in it this time, Robbie-boy." His eyes never left the road, and he did not turn his head away from the windshield. It was like he was talking to someone on the hood of the truck instead of the frightened young man next to him. Robbie said nothing. Even at this early age, he knew that when a highly dominant man like Jake wanted to make a point, there was no value in interrupting or trying to present an alternate point of view. The best strategy was to listen until he was asked to speak, and then if he had to speak, he had better say the right thing.

Jake thought for a minute before speaking again. "So here's the way I see this. You have scared the heck out of your mother, set a terrible example for your brother, disappointed every teacher at your school and made a complete fool of yourself. For my part, I am so mad right now that it is all I can do not to pull this truck over right here and beat you within an inch of your life. The only reason I don't is because I promised your mom I wouldn't hurt you."

Jake's final comment brought two emotions to the top of Robbie's confused psyche. Firstly, he was angry, and in his young man's heart he almost wished his stepfather *would* pull the truck over so he could get a chance to take a few well-deserved swings at Jake. The other emotion he tried to suppress was one of despair. Despite the hatred he felt for Jake and the seriousness of his reckless act, he had hoped that running away would have softened Jake a little, and that he would want to seek to understand why his stepson felt that he needed to get away. Like so many children of broken marriages, he felt out of place and wanted to fit in with his mother and his step father. He wanted Jake's respect, and most of all, he wanted to be loved. He wanted to have a normal life and a chance to have a happy, harmonious home life like so many of his friends. That life was never to be for Robbie Wrigley.

Jake's punishment for Robbie was swift and decisive. His first chore was to move tons of hay bales from one side of the barn to the other by hand, a mammoth task. There was no real need for it, but Jake explained it to Bonnie by telling her that he needed more room to maneuver the tractor. Robbie knew there was no good reason for it, but he put his back into the work and did it without complaint. When his brother Julian tried to go out to the barn to help, Jake grabbed him by the arm and told him to get up to his room and do some homework. "Your brother needs to learn a lesson if he is ever going to amount to anything!" Jake barked. The rough treatment that young Robbie received from Jake was slowly but surely forming his personality and making him into the person he would be as an adult. "I wish I had never been born," Robbie muttered to himself under his breath.

The next three years did not get much better for Robbie, but he stayed on in the Wrigley household until he graduated high school. He saw no point in trying to run away again, so he decided to keep quiet and make the best of it. The day after graduation, he went out looking for work. Bill Johnson had recently hung a help-wanted sign in the window of the Lexington Joshua's Tire Shop, and Robbie decided that because he had fixed so many tires for Jake, he was a bit of an expert at it. He didn't really care what the job was just as long as he had enough money for rent and groceries. Bill knew Jake Wrigley and assumed that any boy who grew up with a successful rancher like him would have to have learned some good values. He found Robbie outgoing and affable, so he hired him on the spot. That was the beginning of a shooting-star career for Robbie. He vowed not to return to Jake Wrigley's ranch and committed himself to the possibility of never seeing his family again.

* * *

Robbie liked being the Sackville branch manager for Joshua's Tires. It gave him the sense of independence and belonging that he had been seeking most of his life. The older workers had some trouble with the fact that Robbie was only twenty-two years old when he came in as the manager, but when they realized that he knew what he was doing, their respect grew and things went fairly well. He was a tough boss, but he rolled up his sleeves and helped whenever help was needed. That gained him a lot of points with the guys in the shop. He was abrupt with them and occasionally overtly rude, but the men just chalked it up to the impetuousness of youth and laughed it off. Robbie had never learned about empathy and compassion at home, so it did not come naturally to him in his new leadership position. Fortunately, none of the other men in the shop had aspirations beyond their current positions, so Robbie had no competition for his job.

Robbie had a natural desire to win, and he knew that success in any business included growth. If he was to impress Walter Kennedy, he would have to increase sales and keep expenses in line so that his profitability could move from mediocre to great. He honed his skills by reading business books, going to seminars and taking courses after work. He learned about marketing, sales and administration, and he learned that if he applied these "hard skills" he could increase sales and improve profitability. He became the salesman, accountant, shop foreman and CEO of the Sackville operation. Within three years, the bottom line of his branch had doubled, and Walter Kennedy was beginning to take notice of Robert Wrigley.

Robbie received several performance awards from Joshua's Tires during his time in Sackville and had been honored by the Sackville Chamber of Commerce as the community's overall best business person two years running. Robbie Wrigley was becoming the golden boy at Joshua's Tires, and it was time for him to move up the ladder.

"Hi there, Robbie!" Walter said enthusiastically when Robbie picked up the phone.

Recognizing his unmistakable voice, Robbie responded, "Well hello, Walter. To what do I owe this unexpected honor?" Walter seldom called his managers without some sort of advance warning, so Robbie's curiosity was piqued.

"Well, Robbie, as you know, we have a number of older managers in the company who will be retiring soon. So I can be comfortable that we have some good succession planning in place, I am looking for some bright young guys like you to start moving up in our organization. With that in mind, I wanted to give you a call to see if you are at all interested in leaving Sackville," Walter stated in a light but serious tone.

Robbie didn't have to think about it. "Oh yes, Walter. I am ready to go any time. I think you know that I want to advance in the company, and I know I can't do it in Sackville. I am ready to do anything you want me to," he said with conviction.

That conversation began a new era in the life of Robbie Wrigley. A few months after the call from Walter, he was moved back to Lexington to replace Bill Johnson in a shop that had twenty employees. Although he again had trouble with morale in the shop, he managed to drive the numbers up and won yet another performance award from Joshua's Tires. He spent the next two years making the Lexington shop one of the top profit makers in the company. Robbie had boundless drive and determination. It was as though every day at work provided him with an opportunity to show Jake Wrigley that he was better than Jake ever thought he could be. He really didn't care too much about how he would get to the top. He just felt he had to get there. His workers were tools in his hands just as he had been a tool for Jake during his years on the ranch. Like his stepfather, he seldom said "thank you" or complimented his people on a job well done. The more work they did, the more he piled on. The less they did, the more he pushed. Because of the distance of the branch from head office and the fact that no one talked to Walter or his regional managers about some of the morale issues in Lexington, Robbie's numbers were the only thing that received head office attention. None of the employees would dare go over Robbie's head because he always made it clear that he was not to be questioned and that his word was law in the shop. Robert Wrigley managed by intimidation, and his deliberately hard management style had served him well to that point in his career. However, it would not always be so.

After almost three years in Lexington, the next call Robbie received from Walter left him almost speechless. After the usual pleasantries, Walter got down to business. "Robbie, I need your help in a big way right now," he began. "Gary Coole had a stroke the other day and had to step down from his job as regional vice president of sales in Calgary. We can't wait on this, so if you are interested in the job, let me know. I can give you until tomorrow afternoon to make up your mind. If you don't want it, I will have to find someone else. If you choose to take it, you will receive a significant increase in pay and you will be cut into the executive bonus plan. As an officer of the company, you will be privy to all our insider information, and you will be part of our officers' share purchase plan. You will also be expected to attend quarterly executive committee meetings and participate in determining the overall direction of the company. This is a great job, Robbie. Are you up to it?"

Robbie sat back in his chair and thought momentarily about what he had just heard. This was his dream. This was his shot at the big time. He didn't have to wait until the next day to make up his mind. He knew what he had to do. "Holy cow, Walter!" he exclaimed. "Of course I want the job. My God, this is what I have always dreamed of. To be part of your executive committee and to run the sales department for the whole region is almost more than I can imagine. And yes, I do think I am up to it! I can hardly wait to get started!"

"That's great, Robbie! I will have Joel call you to get things going. There will be the usual logistics and, of course, some paperwork. Joel is my top guy though, and he will have you moved in and running things in no time. I will come out and see you in couple of weeks to give you some ideas about what I would like to see happen in the Southern Alberta region. So unless you have any questions for me right now,

I need to get down to Dallas and make sure everything is going okay there. Did you know that we were opening up in Texas, Robbie? I am pretty excited about that," Walter said with enthusiasm.

"No, Walter, I did not hear about Texas. That sure is exciting though. Wow, you are really making things happen. It will be so great for me to be on the executive committee and be part of it all!" Robbie said excitedly.

"Welcome aboard, son," Walter said in a comforting tone before excusing himself and hanging up.

The increase in pay he received was more than he expected, and Robbie wasted no time moving to Calgary and buying his first house. That was a momentous day for Robert Wrigley. Here he was not yet thirty years old, a vice president of one of the most important tire retailers on the continent, and moving into a brand new house. "Life doesn't get any better than this!" he thought to himself.

Before Robbie was able to get established in his new role, Walter Kennedy came out to Calgary and spent a day going over the financial statements and business plans for the region. He brought Brad Wilson, the vice president of operations for the region, into the meeting to assist him in going over the statistics. The three men went into Robbie's new office, and Brad laid a huge stack of statements for all of the current and prior year regional financial results on the desk.

Several hours later, when the men had finished reviewing the technicalities of the region, Walter turned to Robbie and said, "These are just numbers, Robbie. What you really need to understand are the *people* issues. People are the secret to your future success or failure here.

Brad is an excellent leader of people. He can help you understand what makes these folks tick and how to get the best out of them. You need to work arm in arm with him to make things happen. Essentially, you and he are partners, so you need to get along, and you must make decisions that work for the both of you. You have equal status in the region, so let's not have any ego issues getting in the way of growth and profitability."

Ignoring Walter's comments, Robbie said, "From what I have seen in these reports, Walter, it looks like I need to push a lot harder with our people to improve sales. I can see now that I created much better margins in both Lexington and Sackville than most of the other offices in the region." Walter noticed that Robbie spoke with a slightly arrogant tone, and that made him uncomfortable.

"Don't confuse high return in short spurts with sustainable profitability, Robbie. You did pull out some great improvements in your last two postings, but that kind of rapid growth is usually not sustainable over the long term. Your people need to be able to work at an acceptable pace in order to remain happy in their jobs. Happy people are productive people. They need to enjoy their work, and they need to believe that they can have fun at work. Make sure you know what is going on in their minds and in their lives before you start to push. We can't afford to lose any of our good people," Walter said sternly.

"Fun? I wonder what he means by *having fun at work*," Robbie thought to himself before responding to Walter. "I never heard any complaints about my way of getting things done in the past, Walter. So I think we will be okay."

"Were you actually listening, Robbie?" Walter asked with a smile.

"I think so. I always found that when I needed something done, it got done, so my people must have been listening," Robbie stated confidently.

"I hope so, Robbie. This is a big job and I need to know that you are up to it. I won't micro-manage you, but I will expect great returns and good morale. Make me proud, and if you have any problems at all, let me know. I am here to help." With that Walter shook Robbie's hand, said good bye to Brad Wilson, and left the building on his way to the airport. Robbie and Brad were suddenly left alone to deal with the business of the entire region and each other.

As soon as Walter left the room, Robbie turned to Brad saying, "I don't know what the heck is going on around here, but I am pretty disappointed in the margins in most of our offices, Brad. What in the world have you and Gary Coole been doing with the people in this region for the past five years? It looks to me like the two of you have been letting the staff do whatever they want instead of making them work. This region should be capable of much better returns than it has now. And let me tell you something: a new day has dawned. I intend to make some changes in this region to get us back on track. If we can't start making some better margins, heads will roll!"

Brad was taken aback by Robbie's tirade and the tone of his voice. He only knew Robbie from having met him at management conferences and various training seminars. In those settings, he found Robbie quite friendly and affable. He had also found Robbie overly confident and a little pushy when the subject of management came up, but like the employees in Sackville, he chalked it up to youth and inexperience. Now he was beginning to worry. Brad was forty-five years old and had been in the operations field for nineteen years. He had worked for a variety of firms during his career and was known to be a fair man with a track record of reasonable success and a reputation for being well respected by his employees. He sensed that Robbie's perspective of what a sales manager's job description was might not be in line with the values that Joshua O'Hare and Walter Kennedy had imprinted into the culture of Joshua's Tires. He knew he had to lay down some ground rules.

"Robbie, I think you and I need to understand a few things," Brad began. "Firstly, the margins in this region are bang on with the company average. I agree that better margins are always desirable, but we must make certain that we set fair and reasonable expectations for our people and for ourselves. Secondly, I am not interested in having any heads roll. This region was built on the backs of the people that work here. They are a family, and in essence, we are their parents. I haven't fired any of my kids from my real family, and I am not going to let you fire any of my work family unless there is a darned good reason!" Brad said confidently and with determination.

Robbie sat down behind the desk and glared at Brad. He could feel the anger rising in him. He had an impulse to start yelling but decided to withhold it and say nothing for the moment. Brad said nothing either. He simply stood confidently waiting for a response from Robbie. The younger man could control his anger no longer.

"You know what I think, Brad? I think you are soft on people. I have heard about your reputation for being kind and fair. I have heard that you are a nice guy. I have also heard that everyone *likes* you. Well, I happen to know that people always like a nice, soft manager who doesn't force them to do their jobs. My way is different. My way gets results. We need to let them know who the boss is, and if they don't measure up, we need to keep the pressure on until they improve or until they break down and leave. Either way we win. We don't need to keep a bunch of deadwood hanging around just for the sake of being *nice*. If you haven't got the guts to do it, then let me handle it. I have no problem telling people to do their jobs or sending them down the road if they don't!" When Robbie finished speaking, his face was red and he was out of breath. His uncontrollable outburst of temper had left him momentarily spent.

Brad Wilson was a fair and reasonable man who was truly well liked by almost everyone he met, but he was by no means soft on staff. Nor did he shy away from confrontation. In this case, however, he could see that Robbie was truly angry, and although he didn't understand what was driving the anger, he knew instinctively that a return of outrage would only exacerbate the situation. He decided to change his stance.

"Look, Robbie," Brad began. "I don't want to fight with you. I think we need to spend some time working together before we do anything. Let's just do our respective jobs for the next few weeks and once we both understand how each of us works, we can get together and compare notes. How does that sound?"

"That's fine with me. I am going to spend the next few weeks getting to know everyone so I can figure out how things work in the region. When I have figured that all out, I will call you so we can deal with any problems I might uncover," Robbie said with no discernable inflection in his voice to indicate his underlying intentions.

Concerned that Robbie had left the battle too easily and suspicious of his motives, Brad said, "And remember, you *do not* have the authority to fire or discipline anyone without my approval. I am the operations manager, so any actions of that kind have to flow through me. I will, however, accept your recommendations and am more than happy to discuss anything and everything with you."

"Fine!" Robbie said curtly. With that, Brad gathered up his financial reports and left Robbie's office without another word.

As he watched Brad walk away, Robbie mumbled to himself, "I don't have to fire anyone, Mr. Milquetoast. By the time I am done with them, they will be wishing they had never been born." At that moment, he recalled how he had mumbled, "I wish I had never been born," while he was piling hay for his stepfather, Jake, but he shook it off in order to avoid thinking about those unhappy times.

Robbie spent the next few weeks driving around the region, meeting the managers and having them introduce him to their staffs. They had all heard that he was coming and were curious to meet him. The jungle drums had already started, and several of his new reports had already called both Lexington and Sackville to find out what kind of guy this new sales manager was. What they heard was that he was a guy who knew how to get things done, but that he was a rude, abrupt man who seldom considered any point of view but his own. They had also heard that he had unrealistic expectations for everyone that worked for him. Strangely, they also heard that he had a humorous and charming side from time to time. He was inconsistent, and you never really knew which Robbie you were going to get. He didn't stand a chance. His reputation preceded him, and it was not a good one. He had survived and flourished in the confined environment of a single store, but on a regional basis there were too many people judging and watching him. His career would soon take a turn for the worse.

On his branch visits Robbie would routinely call various staff members away from their jobs and ask them questions about why they did things a certain way. Often he would criticize them about their work and make suggestions for improvement in front of clients and other staff members. He seemed oblivious to common social graces or normal western politeness. His interrogation of staff members concerned and annoyed his managers, but when they let him know they were unhappy, his negativity turned on them in the form of a swift and furious personal attack. He would often let them know only minutes after meeting them that he was unhappy with their results and that he expected an improvement. After only one visit most managers became so intimidated that they hoped they would never have to see him again.

The result of Robbie's effort was that he alienated almost everyone in the region. Managers were so uncomfortable with him that they went into survival mode. They would do almost anything to stay under his radar and avoid his attention. While they were hiding from his scrutiny, they were doing very little else and production was suffering. Employees would cringe whenever Robbie walked into their store. They would pick up the phone to make imaginary phone calls or run to the bathroom whenever they saw him coming. He was a marked man, but he seemed completely oblivious to the fact that no one liked him or how incredibly negative his actions were. He was on a collision course with failure.

After several months, Robbie had gone from being an imposing figure to a laughing stock whom everyone disliked. His managers and the staff of his various branches made jokes about him behind his back. They imitated his voice, his walk and his mannerisms. They humored him when he asked about sales issues but avoided him as much as possible. He was not invited into office conversations, and he was not asked along to staff social events. Robbie began to feel very alone. He also began to resent Brad Wilson because it was apparent that Brad was very well liked, and because of that he often had managers and staff members in his office looking for advice. He also noticed that people were always smiling when they left Brad's office.

"They should be coming to see me about improving sales instead of wasting time talking to him about administration!" Robbie thought to himself. "Why does everyone want to hang around with a wimp like Brad? I just don't get it." Despite Brad's obvious success with employee relationships, Robbie could not bring himself to become more like Brad or even ask for his advice. He was determined to do things his way. Robbie had been so out of touch with the concept of positive reinforcement all of his life that he could not recognize it when it was right in front of him. Brad was simply being positive with the employees at Joshua's, and that was what made him successful. He was a proponent of *positive passion*, and people sought him out to feel its warmth.

Worst of all, Robbie realized that the financial results he was trying to achieve were not materializing. The bottom line in his region had grown slightly, but it was nowhere near the growth he had hoped for. At the current rate of growth, he would be lucky to make his sales budget for the year. He decided to call a managers' meeting to get things back on track. He had his assistant arrange an all-day meeting at the Stampede Hotel in downtown Calgary. All the branch managers and supervisors in the region were summoned to attend. Robbie did not invite Brad Wilson to attend this meeting. When Brad asked about it, Robbie described it as "strictly a sales meeting" that would not touch on any operational matters, so there was no need for him to attend.

Brad was suspicious, and although he would have liked to attend, he had already planned to meet with the accounting staff that day so he did not protest. In reality, Robbie was so jealous of Brad's relationships with the managers that he wanted to have them all to himself in hopes they would switch allegiance and become *Robbie-disciples*. That was not to be.

After the managers had filed into the room, exchanged greetings and charged their coffee cups, Robbie called the meeting to order. "Okay, folks, let's get on with it. I have a lot to do and only a day in which to do it, so quiet down and listen up!" he said in a loud, stern voice.

"Where's Brad Wilson?" Ron Fredericks from the Lacombe branch yelled from the back of the room.

"Brad didn't want to come," Robbie lied. "He said he had something more important to do than meet with you guys." Robbie's sarcastic comment was a deliberate attempt to discredit his popular counterpart. Neither Ron nor anyone else in the room believed Robbie. Brad had been at every manager's meeting there had been since his arrival in Calgary five years prior. Everyone knew he would not have avoided it if he had been invited. Robbie's attempt to discredit Brad had backfired on him, and the repercussions of his lie would set the tone for the meeting.

Ron Fredericks leaned over to Reg Unrah next to him and whispered, "This guy is really full of it. He probably killed Brad and buried his body under the tire shop." The remark caused Reg to break into laughter, which got Ron laughing to the point that he could not stop.

"Hey, hey, hey, you guys! This is a business meeting. If you have something to say, say it to the group!" Robbie yelled at the two men who by this point were grasping their faces in an effort to stifle their laughter.

Even though he had not heard Ron's comment, Robbie was mad now and decided he was going to get the respect of these people one way or another. He made an instinctive decision to take a hard line in order to show that he meant business.

"Alright ladies and gentlemen, I want to start by telling you that there is not one manager in this room that is hitting the goals I set for you. Not one! This is a huge disappointment to me, and frankly, I don't think Walter Kennedy is going to be very happy about the results you are all turning in." With that comment Robbie paused and looked around the room. Faces were blank. If a pin had been dropped it would have been heard by all. This gave Robbie a powerful feeling of victory, so he carried on.

"So let's go branch by branch and line by line to see why you probably won't make your budgets this year." Robbie said as he switched on the overhead projector next to him. That began a critical and unrelenting dissection of the financial results of each and every branch in the region. Almost every time Robbie hit the button on his remote control, advancing to another page of the financial statement, he would groan in disgust. When he started on a new branch, he would ask the manager to stand up and identify himself. This attempt to embarrass the managers was very successful. After they had identified themselves, he would tell the group how poorly their branch was performing, then do a forecast of how far behind budget they would be if they continued on at their current rate of sales. Each manager fell victim to Robbie's sharp tongue in order of their branch identity numbers. Each felt dread when they knew their turn was coming.

When Robbie got to Ron Fredericks' branch, he said, "So, funny-man, lets see how badly you are doing." Ron's branch was actually well over budget year-to-date and was tracking to have a great year. Nevertheless, Robbie felt the need to make his point. "This is an example of a branch that can easily fail. If Ron here doesn't start taking things seriously, this branch will go right down the toilet. It looks good now, but there is no guarantee that it will stay that way." With that, the walls of the room seemed to shudder from the resounding groan that came out of the audience. Robbie had finally gone too far. Ron Fredericks was the single most revered manager in the region. His branch had turned in the best overall company results for the ten years he had been running it, and he was one of the most knowledgeable and helpful men in the company. Robbie was not prepared for what happened next.

"That's it, Wrigley!" Ron Fredericks said in a loud voice as he pushed himself back in his chair and stood up. "I am out of here. I don't need you, and I don't need this job. Send my severance check to my summer house at Bighorn Lake and get yourself another manager. If you can!"

Robbie was taken aback, but still full of fight. "Sit down, Ron. You're making a fool of yourself," he said in an authoritative tone. Ron ignored him and strode confidently out of the room. As his back disappeared out the door of the meeting room, Reg Unrah began to clap his hands together. In seconds the entire room was applauding, whistling and cheering Ron as he walked down the hotel hallway and out the door to the parking lot.

Robbie knew he was in trouble but was determined to carry on. As the applause subsided, he said, "Okay, folks, let's see if we can get through the rest of the branches before the day is over." He was deflated and defeated and everyone knew it. They sat quietly and listened for the rest of the afternoon as Robbie reviewed the financial statements. Robbie stopped asking them to stand up and identify themselves, and he made very few comments on the financial statements other than regurgitating the information that appeared on the screen. When it was all over, Robbie thanked them quietly and turned his back to the group as he packed up his laptop, his projector, and his paperwork. No one said goodbye to him, and no one spoke as they filed out of the room.

The next day at work marked the beginning of the end for Robbie Wrigley. He arrived at his office at his usual time of 7:30 AM, marched to his office and turned on his computer. When he opened the inbox on his email screen, he was met with a very disturbing message. It was from Reg Unrah, and it said, "Dear Mr. Wrigley. I can no longer continue on in the employ of Joshua's Tire Centers. Please consider this email as official notice of my immediate resignation. I will advise the human resources department of the details." That was all. No explanation and no niceties. Robbie's head was beginning to spin. He was still shaken from Ron Fredericks' resignation at the meeting yesterday, and he thought this had to be the last straw. But it was not.

At 8:45 AM as he was pondering his next move, Robbie's phone rang. It was John Dickson from the Lethbridge branch. "Hey, Robbie," John said nervously. "I just wanted to tell you that I am giving my notice. My wife has been asking me to retire for years, and you know, after that meeting yesterday, I realized that now is the time."

"John, please don't do it," Robbie said pleadingly.

"Sorry, kid. My mind is made up. You made me see that I am not up to the business anymore, and frankly, after Ron walked out, retirement began to feel right to me. You really blew it there you know," Ron said in a helpful tone.

"John, is there anything I can do to make you change your mind? I really don't want you to go," Robbie pleaded.

"Nope, I'm done. But you had better get that chip off your shoulder and realize that you are nothing without your team. If you expect to keep working for Walter Kennedy, you had better figure that out. Good luck, boy." With that John hung up, and Robbie was left to ponder his future.

Robert Wrigley knew he had to make the call. He really didn't want to talk to Walter Kennedy, but he knew that if he didn't bring him into the loop now, there could be trouble for him later. Robbie knew that Walter was a hands-on kind of guy who would go to bat for anyone who asked for help. He also knew that Walter did not like failure, and as kind as he was, he would not stand for secrecy or deceit from his managers when it came to problems that could have negative effects on the finances of the company. His hands shook as he picked up the phone and dialed Walter Kennedy's number.

"Hello, Walter," Robbie said quietly.

As always, Walter Kennedy offered a friendly, cheerful response. "Well, hello there, Robbie. How are things out there in Calgary today?"

"Not very good, Walter," Robbie began. "I think we have a problem." With that Robbie told him the story of how Ron Fredericks walked out at the meeting, about Reg Unrah's resignation and about John Dickson's phone call. He choked up on several occasions, but he managed to tell the entire story without embellishing or making excuses. He took full responsibility for the resignations of Joshua's best managers and then finished with, "So what do you think, Walter?"

Walter was crushed. Ron, Reg and John were three of his favorite managers. All of them had been with Joshua's for years, and all had turned in handsome profits year after year. He could hardly believe what he was hearing.

"What does Brad Wilson have to say about all of this, Robbie?" Walter asked.

"He doesn't know yet. I haven't told him," Robbie said weakly.

"Well, go and tell him right now and tell him to call me. If anyone can get those guys back, it's Brad. I don't know how you could have let this happen without him being involved in the first place, but I can tell you that I intend to find out. I will be there when you open tomorrow morning, so I hope you can come up with a better explanation than I have heard so far," Walter sputtered.

"I'm sorry, Walter," was all Robbie could get out before he heard the click of Walter's phone on the other end of the line. At that moment he felt the same sick feeling in his stomach that he did that day when his stepfather found him at the pipeline construction camp. He knew something bad was going to happen, but he didn't know what it would be.

When Walter arrived the next morning, Robbie was ready for him. "Hi, Walter. I hope you had a nice trip," he offered.

"The trip was fine," Walter said slowly before getting on with business. "I was back and forth with Brad all day yesterday, and he has managed to get Ron and Reg to come back. John has decided to retire and will not come back under any circumstances. We kind of expected him to retire soon anyway. He is at that age, and your meeting was all he needed to convince him that it was time."

"Well, that's great news about Ron and Reg, anyway. I guess you can't blame me too much for John since he was going to retire anyway. Ha ha," Robbie laughed half-heartedly.

"There is nothing funny here, Robbie. The fact of the matter is that the only way we could get Ron and Reg back was to agree that they would no longer be forced to have anything to do with you," Walter stated calmly.

"Oh," was all Robbie could say as his chin sunk to his chest in despair.

When Walter saw the look of defeat on Robbie's face, his naturally strong sense of empathy came to the forefront of his psyche. He immediately felt the need to make things better for the young man before him. Walter was once a young, struggling manager too, and he knew how hard it was to be great at everything. In this case he also felt a lot of responsibility for Robbie's failure.

"Look, Robbie. I have to tell you that I made a big mistake with you. When I moved you into Sackville as the manager, I should have done an aptitude profile on you, and then when I moved you back to Lexington, I made the same mistake again. My greatest mistake was moving you to Calgary to replace Gary Coole. I should have known what you were capable of before I gave you such a huge responsibility. I have always prided myself on putting the right person in the right job, and this time I didn't follow my own rule. Frankly, I let you down. We were desperate to get someone into place each time, and I went ahead and moved you without knowing if you were up to it."

"But, I think I *was* up to it," Robbie offered.

"No, you weren't, son," Walter said sympathetically. "You simply don't have enough of an understanding of yourself or others yet to make it in management. You have extremely poor social awareness which makes it impossible for you to understand what motivates people or how you should lead them. Even without doing the aptitude profile, I am guessing that you are very insecure and that you are generally down on life. You have a lot of arrogance, though, which makes you believe that people will follow you without question. The biggest problem is that your empathy level is so low while your desire for domination is so high; this makes you come across as quite demeaning. From what I am told, most people find you completely obnoxious. I have seen these characteristics in managers before, and generally we find that something tremendously negative has happened to them at some point in their lives that caused them to become bitter. That bitterness causes them to want to show others that they are better than they really are, and they simply drive people away with their superior, insensitive attitude. Does that sound like you, Robbie?"

Robbie could not speak. Thoughts of his stepfather, Jake, flashed into his mind and he became overwhelmed with depression. He knew he had blown his chance for greatness with Joshua's Tires and felt like running away, just as he had when he was fifteen years old. Unfortunately, this time the pipeline job would not satisfy him as it did in his youth.

He did not know what to do. Fortunately, Walter Kennedy's belief in ***positive passion*** would save Robbie from the oblivion he was hurtling toward.

Knowing that Robbie was not going to answer his last question, Walter began again, "Look, Robbie, I want to put you through the profile process and see where you might fit in our organization. You have worked hard for us and I think we owe you that. What do you think?"

Robbie was still wallowing in depression and self pity, but he understood that Walter genuinely had his best interests at heart. He did not want to leave Joshua's Tires, and he did want to find out more about himself, so he agreed to travel back to Toronto with Walter and go through the profile process with Joel.

When Joel and Walter reviewed the profile, they found that Robbie was as they had suspected, very low on empathy and very high on dominance. He had a negative opinion of the outside world but a very high opinion of himself. He would need some coaching, and they would recommend some professional counseling from a qualified psychologist. They were confident that he could be a great salesperson if he could overcome some of the demons that had been haunting him.

Robbie went on to become a great sales person working out of the new Dallas, Texas, branch of Joshua's Tires. He learned to accept other people for who they are and made many friends. In time, he reunited with his mother, his brother and his stepfather. He married a woman who looked strikingly like his mother, and he raised two boys of his own. ***Positive passion*** saved Robert Wrigley from a life of potential misery.

CHAPTER SIX

Good Leaders Need Good Followers

Coaches who win a lot of games usually have a knack for good player selection…

CHAPTER 6

Good Leaders Need Good Followers

One day as Joel, Bella, and Walter were planning for the coming year over coffee and doughnuts in the boardroom, Joel said, "You know something, Walter, you have had a huge amount of success with your *positive passion* management methods, and I was thinking that you should put together a seminar on it and present it to our managers at the spring leadership conference."

"What a great idea!" Bella chimed. "Everyone is always talking about *positive passion*, but I don't think most of them really understand what it's all about."

Walter thought for a moment before saying, "Hey! How come you guys are picking on me? You are the expert on aptitude profiling, Joel, and Bella, you practice *positive passion* with your sales team everyday. I think you guys should be doing the seminars!"

"Actually, Walter, Bella and I are both on the agenda to do presentations. I will be doing a workshop on aptitude profiling, and Bella will do a session on goal setting and sales management," Joel said with a smile.

"So what do you say now, Walter?" Bella asked with a giggle.

"Well, I guess I am fresh out of excuses, so I suppose I can put something together. How long do you think I will have to speak?"

Joel answered immediately, "Well, it turns out that we have a two-hour time slot right after the welcome speech. And I am thrilled that we managed to get Joshua O'Hare to come out and do the opening speech this year. You know how the managers love to get a chance to rub shoulders with our founding father. I think your session would be a great way to start the conference after Joshua has left the stage. You know, it will set everyone up for a positive time and take the heat off me when I do my session after lunch."

"Always thinking of yourself aren't you, Joel," Walter said with a twinkle in his eye. "I will do my best, but frankly, I haven't done anything like this since my days in the insurance business, so I will probably be quite rusty. But of course, you both knew that. I think you just want me to go first because you expect me to be lousy, and I will make you both look good!"

Joel and Bella erupted into laughter. They had never seen Walter so insecure before. They were both very happy to witness his vulnerability because it made him just that much more likeable. Not that he needed any help in that regard.

"Well, I suppose I had better go back to my office and start writing," Walter mumbled as he got up from the boardroom table and headed out the door.

"He will do great," Bella said confidently to Joel.

"You know it," Joel responded. They both knew that when given any task, Walter Kennedy would work tirelessly to make a success of it.

As Walter made his way back to his office, he contemplated a lot of concepts, ideas and theories. "How should I start this thing? What angle should I take? What will motivate the managers?" he thought. "What kind of information will interest them and how will I hold their attention?" Those thoughts led his mind to various situations and issues he had encountered over the years. Robbie Wrigley appeared briefly in his mind, and he smiled. He thought about what *positive passion* really meant to him and what made an exemplary leader. He knew that his personal passion was to lead by pure, positive energy. He wondered, though, how many of his managers actually shared his vision.

Walter thought about some of the bad characters who had passed through his life and how their negative energy seemed designed to deliberately harm those around them. He remembered Teresa Jameson who almost cost him his job when he was a young insurance manager with Shelton Saunderson.

Teresa was a troubled young lady who suffered from depression and constant mood swings. She would be happy one day and miserable the next. She would be energetic and ambitious for several days in a row and then fall into a period of almost complete idleness during which she would accomplish nothing. She would sometimes want to be everyone's friend, while other times she hated everyone who came into contact with her and had no qualms about telling her co-workers why. She had an overwhelming desire to help those in need, but at times her generosity was replaced by resentment of everyone around her. When she was in a negative mood, she blamed her supervisor and her branch manager for every problem in her life.

Teresa was a bright lady who simply could not get it together. She would often come up with new innovations and different ways to do her job. The problem was that her ideas did not fit the routine at Shelton Saunderson. She was a customer service representative with a very specific job description. The workflows and ways of getting her job done had been established many years before her arrival and worked well for everyone else in her department. However, she wanted to be more creative and do things differently. Her ideas generally tended to cause less work for her and more work for someone else. She wasted so much time trying to do things differently that the work that absolutely needed to get done was beginning to suffer. Whenever she was rebuked by her supervisor, Cher, she would become angry and, ultimately, despondent. She began to believe that Cher had something against her and didn't like her. She made it personal and began a feud in the office. She spoke negatively against Cher to anyone who would listen.

When Teresa finally came to the realization that Cher would never allow her to utilize the ideas she had dreamed up, she went to her manager, Chris. He was an old-school kind of leader who believed that supervisors should supervise and employees should just do as they are told. When Teresa complained to him, he told her to make more of an effort to get along with Cher and stop trying to change things. Teresa left his office, not accepting what she had heard. She continued on her negative path and fought with Cher at every turn. Finally Cher went to Chris and complained about Teresa's attitude. The manager suggested that they simply fire her, but upon further questioning he found that none of Teresa's transgressions had ever been written up and no formal warnings had ever been given. He knew that she could charge the company with wrongful dismissal if they were to let her go. Knowing that the situation had come to the boiling point, he called Walter Kennedy for help.

"Hey, Walter, I've got a problem here, and I am hoping you can give me a hand."

After listening to the manager's story, Walter decided to talk to Teresa himself and see if he could get to the bottom of her problems and help her move into more positive territory. He asked Teresa to come into his office and have a chat with him. True to form, Teresa talked very positively about the innovations she wanted to make to her job description and blamed Cher for her inability to get her job done. She admitted that she had fallen behind in her work but felt that if she were allowed to institute her new innovations, this would improve things to the point that she would be ahead of everyone else.

Walter listened patiently to her until she stopped talking, then pulled out some statistics for her department. He pointed out to her that, on average, she was doing one third less work than everyone else in her department, and that one of her co-workers was actually handling twice as many files as her every month. He then pointed out that all of the other CSR's in her department were using the same workflows and systems and that none of them were unhappy with the way things were done. When Walter finished explaining Teresa's shortfalls to her, he asked what was *really* bothering her.

"You are just like all of the rest of them!" Teresa said through tears that had welled up in her eyes during Walter's lecture. "Everyone in this place is out to get me, and it's all because of that woman!"

"What woman?" Walter asked quietly.

"Cher!" Teresa cried. "She has been going around the office telling people that I am stupid and that I should be fired!" Walter knew that Cher was of the highest character, and she was loved and respected by everyone in the office. He was certain those words would never come from Cher's mouth.

"Now, Teresa, why would she do that?" Walter asked in a kindly tone.

"I don't know. I think she hates me!" she cried again.

"You know what, Teresa, I think you are in the wrong job. Frankly, I think you are in over your head, and I don't think this has anything to do with Cher at all. I would like to move you into a different position in a different department and see how things work out for you there. What do you think about that idea?" Walter offered.

Teresa thought for a moment as she wiped the tears from her eyes and blew her nose. "I think this is extremely unfair. This is not all my fault, and I think you are blaming me completely for everything that went wrong because you have a thing going on with that woman!"

"Pardon me?" Walter asked in a surprised and irritated manner.

"Nothing, nothing," Teresa said in a dismissive tone.

"Look, Teresa, attacking me won't help you either. You have to accept that you have not been keeping up with your job, and I am now offering you a chance to try something different that better suits your skills. Do you want the job or not?" Walter asked sternly.

"Fine!" Teresa snapped. "Are you done with me now?"

Walter was totally perplexed by Teresa's attitude and really could not imagine what she was thinking. "How could she justify such abhorrent behavior; how could she think that her work was acceptable or that everyone else was to blame for her poor performance?" he thought as she walked away.

Teresa left Walter's office, never to return to Shelton Saunderson again. Instead of taking the new job Walter had offered, she wrote a letter of resignation along with a complaint of harassment against Walter and Cher. In her letter she accused them of treating her differently than other employees and of conspiring to get rid of her by destroying her reputation with other staff members. In her letter she also accused Walter and Cher of having a romantic affair which was allegedly known to the majority of the staff members.

As Shelton Saunderson took harassment of any kind extremely seriously, they launched an investigation which Walter feared might end his career. Of course since both he and Cher were individuals of the highest character, and since there were no facts to indicate that they had harassed Teresa in any way, they were both exonerated.

Walter Kennedy learned the value of a good reputation during that unfortunate time, and also that no matter how positive you are, it is wise to be very cautious when dealing with unhappy employees.

Positive passion will not work with someone who has serious psychological or emotional problems. Walter believed that in those rare cases, it is best to keep your distance and deal with the employee in a completely businesslike and professional fashion. Always take notes of every conversation and have witnesses present in the event of any serious discussions. Fortunately, Walter did not have to suffer any similar attacks for the balance of his career, but he never forgot Teresa Jameson. She momentarily shook his belief system and taught him that no matter how good a leader is, he or she cannot lead people who steadfastly refuse to follow. Good leaders will shake off a singular failure, however, and move on to more positive results.

As Walter's mind drifted away from Teresa, he recalled a nasty situation during his first year at Joshua's Tires when harassment *did* exist.

Ron Gordon was a manager in a small town in Northern Ontario, sixty miles north of Spruce River where Walter had grown up. He was a few years younger, but Walter knew of him during his adolescent years. He was infamous in the area as a mischievous trouble maker.

After leaving high school, Ron had gone through the ranks at Joshua's Tires as a flat fixer and tire installer. After a few years of that, he moved into sales. In no time at all, he proved to be a great sales person. The same drive to be the center of attention that carved out his reputation as a trouble maker also made him a natural sales person. Every sales opportunity provided him with a stage where he could show off, be funny, and *win*. Customers generally liked his enthusiasm and his raw desire to be successful. They bought from him because he impressed them with his need to make the sale. He managed to convince his customers that they needed whatever he had to sell and that he was the best person to provide it. In a few short years, he was turning in the best sales numbers in the company, and he was making a great living for himself.

Although Ron had made the transition from adolescent to adult without getting into any serious trouble, he never lost his desire to be the center of attention, and he always found that being politically incorrect and insulting garnered him more attention than simple humor. It certainly got him more laughs than being kind or supportive ever did. He entered every situation looking for a chance to shine as a force to be reckoned with and a leader to be admired.

In addition to being politically incorrect in almost every situation Ron was quite a ladies' man. He was good looking and, not surprisingly, he had a way with women. In his peer group the more conquests a young man could make, the more he was admired. Gaining the admiration of others was Ron's central driving force, so he set out to be the greatest lover since Casanova. He felt nothing for the girls he conquered. Each one was another notch in his gun, and each sexual encounter was reenacted by Ron to his friends in great detail. He never gave a thought to the harm he might be doing to the girls he was gossiping about. All he thought about was how much he must be admired as he regaled his young male friends with detailed stories of his encounters. He was a stereotypical male chauvinist with no respect or regard for the opposite sex beyond their ability to satisfy his physical and emotional needs.

When Ron was thirty years old, his philandering ways came to a shuddering halt when one of his conquests announced to him that she was pregnant. Although shocked, fearful, and angered by this encroachment on his bachelorhood, Ron was intrigued by the prospect of having a baby. He liked the idea of having a son to emulate him in every way. The thought of having a daughter never entered his mind.

Grudgingly, Ron married Brenda in a civil ceremony at the court house in Spruce River. There was no reception party, and only Ron's brother and Brenda's parents attended the ceremony. Three months later, little Jeremy Gordon was born. One year later Brenda filed for divorce, citing irreconcilable differences. Ron did not enjoy the married life. He was seldom home, and although he was true to his vows, he hated the confinement of marriage and longed for the single life.

Ron did not object to the divorce but what he had not considered was that Brenda would want fifty percent of everything he owned, child support for Jeremy, and alimony payments for herself. This would put Ron into a negative financial situation that would not abate until Jeremy grew up and left home. As the divorce case continued on through the courts, Ron became more and more hateful of Brenda, and his lack of respect for the female gender became even more deeply ingrained.

Ron had become a branch manager at Joshua's Tires a year prior to his marriage to Brenda. Joshua O'Hare was not aware of Ron's true character but was very aware of his sales success. He felt that anyone who could sell like Ron could teach others how to sell as well. When he met with Ron to discuss his promotion, he found Ron quite affable and outgoing. Ron was smart enough to keep his usual political incorrectness to himself during that meeting, so from Joshua's perspective Ron was perfect for the job. It would not be long before Joshua began to regret his decision, but fortunately for him, he had recently taken Walter Kennedy on as his Chief Operations Officer so he was able to avoid the drama that was about to unfold.

Unbeknownst to Joshua or Walter, Ron had become more negative toward the opposite sex than he had ever been in his entire life. He had moved from *ladies' man* to *woman hater* since his divorce. He now looked at the females working in his branch as lesser creatures that could do nothing right. They were beings to be used for simplistic and unimportant tasks only. They should not advance, and they should not be paid as much as men regardless of their skill or output. Ron would only offer simple politeness to his female staff and nothing more. When he spoke with any of the men in the branch, he was more than happy to involve himself in sexist remarks and put-downs of any female that happened to enter the conversation. Discussions of a sexual nature were common place. Some of those discussions got back to the female members of his staff, and a pall was gradually cast over Ron's ability to manage as the women in the branch became more and more aware of his prejudice against them. Ultimately he gained a well-deserved reputation as a male chauvinist who did not respect the women who worked for him. Those same women longed to see his demise.

Finally one day *it* happened. Ron went too far. A young woman named Hannah Borden was hired by the front end supervisor in Ron's branch as a customer service representative. Some of the men in the shop had commented to Ron that she had a great body and wasn't too hard to look at. Ron made a special trip out of his office at the back of the shop to find out what he had been missing. He walked right up to Hannah, looked her up and down from head to toe, winked at her and said in a lascivious tone, "Not baaaaad!" With that he nodded to the front end manager, Mary Belafonte, and walked away without even bothering to address Hannah directly. Hannah looked embarrassed as Mary watched Ron heading toward the service shop to discuss Hannah's physical characteristics with the guys in the shop. His were the acts of a chauvinistic, thoughtless, self-centered boor, and Mary was not going to let him get away with it.

Mary Belafonte had worked hard in a man's world to move up to her position as a front end manager at Joshua's Tires. Joshua was very proud of her progress in his company and had slated her for senior management in the future. Her job in Ron's shop was the stepping stone to running her own branch. Because she knew Joshua and Walter quite well and trusted them to do the right thing, she wasted no time in calling Walter to tell him about Ron's most recent faux pas.

"Hi, Walter. I hate to call you about stuff like this, but Ron has simply gone too far this time!" she sputtered into the telephone.

"What's up, Mary?" Walter asked in a kindly tone. He knew that Mary would not call him with a problem unless it was something very serious. "So tell me what Ron has done to upset you."

"Oh, Walter, the guy is just such a pig toward women!" Mary blurted, before launching into an extremely accurate story of Ron's behavior toward Hannah.

When Mary finished recounting the event, Walter asked, "Is this new behavior, or has Ron been like this all along?"

"Well, he has always been an overt male chauvinist, but since he split up with his wife he has been unbelievably bad. He spends a lot of time hanging around the service bays talking dirty with the other men, and he even tells disgusting sexual jokes to me. He seems to be totally focused on sex, but that is not the real problem. The thing that bothers me is that he is so negative toward women in general. If he is not talking dirty about them, he is running them down. He is bad news, and none of the women in this branch want to have anything to do with him, Walter. The problem is that he is the boss here, and the only way we can get away from him is to quit. And don't think a lot of us aren't considering that, too!" Mary said, clearly flustered.

Without hesitation Walter said, "I will be there in the morning, Mary. Does Ron know that you are calling me?"

"No, he doesn't, but I don't care. Go ahead and tell him. I am sick of him, and if I have to keep working for Ron Gordon, I won't be here long anyway," Mary said, sounding defeated.

"Are you making a formal complaint of sexual harassment, Mary?" Walter asked.

Mary thought for a moment. "Well, yes, as a matter of fact, I am," she answered confidently.

"Don't do anything rash, Mary. I will make this right," Walter said in a kindly tone.

When Walter walked into Ron Gordon's Joshua's Tires branch the next morning, he had no idea how his visit would end. Nor did he know exactly what he was going to say to Ron. He only knew that he had to confirm Mary's story, and if it was as bad as she had described it, he would have to take some serious action. He wasn't looking forward to the next few hours.

Ron looked very surprised to see Walter Kennedy walking into his office. "Hey, Walter, what brings you here?" he asked nervously, shooting his hand toward Walter in order to enable an obligatory handshake. The two men shook hands briefly, looking into each other's eyes, both wondering what might come next.

After exchanging meaningless pleasantries, Walter went right to the heart of matter, "So, Ron, tell me what you think of Hannah?" he asked glibly.

"What do you mean?" Ron asked, confused by the question.

Thinking on the fly, Walter countered with, "Well, as I was walking through the shop, I overhead one of the guys commenting on her *form*." Walter looked Ron in the eyes and smiled. As he assumed that Walter was interested in chatting about Hannah's physical attributes, Ron began a lengthy dissertation about the form and dimensions of the young lady in question. Walter quickly grew tired of Ron's disgusting, sexually charged remarks and decided to find out how deeply Ron's prejudice really ran.

"So how much are we paying her, Ron?" Walter interrupted.

"Ah, well, she's new here, so we started her at a thousand bucks a month, like we do all the girls."

Walter could not stop his eyebrows from rising at that comment. "Right. And how much do we start men at in this branch?" Walter asked quietly.

Ron was quick to answer, "Well, Walter, you can't compare the two, can you? This is a tire shop. It's a man's business. I know we have to hire a few of these little *Twinkies* to make the do-gooders and the politicians happy, but we sure as heck don't have to pay them as much." Walter could hardly believe what he was hearing, but he wanted to see how far Ron would go with this line of thought.

"Really, Ron. I am quite interested in your views of women in the workforce. Tell me more."

Assuming Walter was a kindred spirit, Ron spoke with the enthusiasm of someone who had just won an award. "Well, we both know that women are being forced on us by the government and various politically-correct groups around the country. I suppose it started with Women's Lib in the sixties, but it is getting out of control. These broads want to take over our jobs without actually doing the work that men do, and people like us have to stop it from happening. I am sick to death of them getting jobs that should go to men just because they are women. I let Mary have her way and hire a woman from time to time, but there is no way I am going to let her think they are equal to men."

"So tell me something, Ron. If Hannah took an apprenticeship and became a journeyman mechanic, would you consider putting her into a shop foreman's job?"

"Not a chance, Walter. Who would listen to her? She would just be a skirt with mechanic's papers. Those guys out there would laugh her into the next century!" With that Ron actually laughed out loud.

Walter had heard enough. He decided it was time to let Ron in on the reason for his visit. "Ron, I have received a complaint of sexual harassment against you, and it involves Hannah. I need you to focus on the gravity of this complaint and tell me what happened between you and Hannah yesterday," he said calmly, yet strongly.

Ron almost jumped out his chair. "What are you talking about? I can't believe this crap, Walter. I did nothing to her! What has she said about me? Whatever it is, I can get witnesses who will say that it's a load of crap!" Ron sat back and waited for a response. His face was red, his fists were clenched and a vein was visibly throbbing in his forehead.

"Hannah said nothing about you, Ron. The complaint was brought by Mary Belafonte," Ron answered.

"That makes no sense at all. I have never harassed Mary." Realizing his error, Ron added, "What I mean is I have never harassed anyone. What in the world is Mary mad about? This is all crazy," he mumbled, slumping back in his chair.

"Please understand that essentially anything that someone does or says that offends or harms another person psychologically or emotionally in the workplace can be considered harassment. In this case, the harassment is of a sexual nature against someone of the opposite gender, Ron, and therefore it is sexual harassment. You do not have to harass Mary directly in order for her to bring a charge of harassment against you. Having said all of that, I must tell you that I have also been made aware of sexually offensive comments and jokes that you made directly to Mary. Why don't you tell me what happened with Hannah yesterday, Ron?" Walter asked softly.

Strangely enough, Ron recounted the story of his encounter with Hannah almost exactly as it happened. He was confident that since the only words he uttered were, "Not bad," he had done nothing wrong, and therefore nobody should find fault with him. Walter advised him that his words, his actions, his comments to the men in the shop, his sexual comments and jokes to Mary along with his generally negative attitude toward women all made it clear that he was guilty of sexual harassment on a large scale. Walter knew he could not leave this situation without a significant show of management support for those individuals Ron had victimized.

"Ron, although this is clearly not your first offense, it is the first time I have talked to you about it. That being the case, I am not going to terminate you today. However, I cannot possibly consider leaving you in charge here, and I will be writing you up. A letter of admonishment will go into your file and will form a permanent part of your record with our company. Any future events of a similar nature will result in further discipline up to and including termination," Walter said sternly.

Knowing that Walter was serious, Ron spoke softly, "Well, I can see you have your mind made up. I suppose there is nothing more I can say, is there? So who is going to run the place and what will I be doing?"

Walter thought for a moment before saying, "I am going to move Mary into your position as manager. You will be moved into the shop as foreman. The current foreman, Ryan, has been asking for a transfer to Toronto anyway, so it all works out," Walter stated matter-of-factly.

"Works out! You call that working out? If you think I am going to work for a woman after everything I have said to you, you must be nuts. This is just wrong, and on top of that it is nothing less than insulting. I am not going to take this, Walter! If you do this, I am out of here!" Ron screamed. He was red in the face again and standing up behind his desk now.

Undeterred, Walter said, "I have made my decision. If you really feel the need to quit, then that will be your decision. Let me know what you want to do." Walter stood his ground and gazed into Ron's eyes while awaiting his response. He could see the tears of anger and fear welling up in the man he had just disciplined, and yet he did nothing. He wanted to help him, but he could not back down now. Ron had set up a situation from which there was no turning back, and Walter had to choose the integrity of the company and its employees over his compassion for this man.

Ron's face suddenly took on the appearance of someone twenty years older as he turned away from Walter and got out of his chair. Without a word he walked past Walter, through the shop, and into the parts room. Walter wondered what was going on. In seconds Ron returned from the parts room with a cardboard box in his hand. He marched into his office, brushing past Walter and began emptying the contents of his desk and various shelves and cabinets in the office into the box. Walter watched him without speaking.

When Ron had retrieved all his personal items, he turned to Walter and said, "There you go, Boss. You can take this job and shove it! Let the women take it over. I am done with you!" With that he marched out to the parking lot, got into his immaculately restored 'sixty-nine Dodge Charger and drove away.

As Walter's mind snapped back to the current day, again he thought about *positive passion* and how it simply cannot work on someone who is totally determined to be negative to the detriment of themselves and everyone around them.

In the case of both Teresa Jameson and Ron Gordon, even though abhorrent behavior was evident and disengagement was obvious, Walter wanted to provide options in order to allow his employees an opportunity to improve. Often when confronted with the knowledge that management is aware of disengagement and toxic behavior, the guilty employee will quit in order to retain some semblance of personal integrity. Leaving also allows them the luxury of blaming management for their demise, and criticizing the former employer at every turn takes the focus away from their own failure.

Walter never worried about criticism from former employees. His own integrity was strong, and he knew that anyone who resigned on bad terms had been given a fair chance to improve. He also knew that people who exhibit abhorrent behavior at work often live a life of misery and have very few people in their lives who take their negativity seriously.

Even though he was willing to give Teresa and Ron a second chance, he accepted that there are times when ***positive passion*** should not be utilized. Criminal acts and physical abuse in the workplace for example, must not be tolerated. Walter winced as he thought back on a situation that hurt him deeply.

Because of his strong leadership skills and natural charisma, Walter was fortunate to have a number of former employees from his insurance days at Shelton Saunderson follow him to Joshua's Tires. One of those employees was Sarah Jones. He first met Sarah when he was a young branch manager at Shelton Saunderson in Toronto. She was friendly, bright, and receptive but quite reserved. She was a single mother who lived a meager existence on her clerk's salary. She had no life beyond her children and her work. She dressed poorly and seldom attended company functions. She was not fortunate enough to acquire an education beyond high school and did not have the time or resources to improve herself through correspondence courses or night school. She was doomed to a life of subsistence. Although Walter quite liked Sarah, she tended to work quietly behind the scenes and blended into obscurity in almost everything she did. Because of her virtual invisibility, Walter seldom thought about her. When she applied to Joshua's Tires after Walter had taken over from Joshua O'Hare, he was pleased to see her and hired her on the spot. He placed her in an administrative position in the Joshua's Tires Oakville shop, and true to form Sarah blended into the woodwork and was forgotten again for three years…until one day when the unthinkable happened.

During a routine audit by the company's accountants it was discovered that the Oakville shop had shorted its bank account by approximately five thousand dollars over the course of the previous year. The auditors had difficulty sorting out exactly where the money had gone, but after a good deal of forensic accounting, they realized that the missing amount was the result of a complicated series of invoicing irregularities and corresponding bank deposit manipulations. Once they realized what had occurred, they dug deeper and found that these were not errors but instead appeared to be a well-planned attempt to remove small amounts of cash from a large number of bank deposits over a nine-month period. This was obviously an inside job, and their next task was to determine which Joshua's employee was embezzling the money. Having had some experience with this type of thing in the past, the auditors worked out a scheme with Walter to set up a sting operation to find out who the guilty party was. In a very short time, the auditors had eliminated the branch manager, the front line manager and all other staff who had access to cash…except Sarah Jones. The next step was to set up a fake invoicing situation and a bank deposit to see if Sarah would alter the records and take some cash.

Walter could not believe his ears when the auditors told him that Sarah Jones was the embezzler they had been looking for. He demanded to see all the evidence for himself, hoping to find something to prove them wrong and exonerate this poor lady. Life had served her up a series of hardships already, and this situation, if she were guilty, would be devastating to her and her children. He stayed up most of the night poring over the records, but he was unable to uncover anything to refute the auditors' findings and had to admit to himself that Sarah was guilty.

Weary from his night of research and with a heavy heart, Walter pulled into the parking lot of the Oakville branch the next morning. After parking his car, he walked directly into the manager's office and asked him to call Sarah into the office. When she arrived at the door, Walter waived her in without speaking. Sarah was visibly nervous, and Walter was clearly agitated. Sarah feared what might be coming next, and Walter feared that he might break down while doing the job he hated the most.

"How are you, Sarah?" he asked in a kindly tone.

"I'm fine, Mr. Kennedy," she responded meekly.

Walter steeled himself, set his mind to the job at hand and matter-of-factly described the process the auditors had gone through to lead them to this moment in time. Sarah said nothing and did not react, nor did she look Walter in the eye throughout his explanation. Finally her silence was broken by a question from Walter.

"Sarah, the auditors tell me that everything points to the fact that you must have taken this money. I have reviewed everything in detail, and as much as I hate to say it, I have to agree with their findings. Did you take it?" he asked calmly.

Sarah did not look up. She had been staring at an imaginary object on the floor for several minutes and almost seemed paralyzed. Walter waited patiently. Finally, without looking up, she spoke. "No," was all she said.

Feeling frustrated, Walter responded with, "Well, okay then, Sarah. I guess you have two choices here. If you admit that you took the money, I will simply terminate your employment with us for cause. If on the other hand, you continue to deny that you had any involvement in it, I will have to call in the police to do a full investigation. If you are found guilty, you will be prosecuted criminally, and you might have to do some jail time."

Sarah, still staring at the floor began to weep silently. The tears ran down her face and dripped onto her well-worn white cotton blouse.

Walter was barely able to control himself, but he stayed silent. The branch manager, who had been in the room the entire time, had not said a word, but now felt compelled to fill the silence. "Sarah, don't let this happen to you. Please don't let this happen to your children!" he pleaded.

The emotion in the room was palpable. It was like a funeral for a loved one. It was a horrible moment for everyone there.

Finally Sarah lifted her tear-streaked face and made the statement that no one wanted to hear. "I did it, Mr. Kennedy. I did it for my kids." With that she put her face in her hands and sobbed uncontrollably. Walter could not ignore her pain and put his arm gently around Sarah's shoulder, squeezing her arm gently in a gesture of emotional support.

As difficult as it was, Walter terminated Sarah's employment that day. Despite the comparatively small amount of money and Sarah's personal situation, he could not allow embezzlement to be excused. As much as he wanted to employ *positive passion* along with discipline and reinforcement, he knew that he had only one choice. Unfortunately Sarah's indiscretion was too great, even for Walter Kennedy.

There are some indiscretions that may not be excused. The best leaders know that to allow embezzlement, assault, simple theft, fraud, vandalism or other criminal acts to be tolerated without swift and decisive action is to allow chaos to reign in the workplace. Criminal acts, no matter how minor, must be dealt with harshly as soon as they are discovered in order to deter others from such acts and to set an example for the future. To ignore these situations would be to eliminate all corporate integrity and allow the company to share in the guilt.

A month after Sarah had been dismissed from Joshua's Tires, she was delighted and amazed to find that an anonymous individual had deposited ten thousand dollars into her personal bank account. She tried to find out who had made this incredible contribution to her life but was never able to locate her benefactor. Walter had sworn the bank manager to secrecy.

One of Walter's greatest challenges was teaching his managers to be leaders. Many people have the knowledge and technical skills to manage the nuts and bolts of a business, but only a few have the natural ability to manage people. Managing people is not about managing timelines and staffing levels. It is all about leadership and passion. People management is the most important element of modern business, yet managers keep making the same age-old mistakes over and over again. Walter's mind wandered to one of his older managers who, despite

Walter's coaching, could not break out of the stereotypical manager role and develop a leadership mentality.

Stan Harper was a fifty-year old shop foreman whom Walter promoted to branch manager in one of the largest Joshua's Tires shops when the previous manager retired. Stan had been in the tire business most of his adult life and knew everything there was to know about keeping a tire shop running. He had done every job in the shop except branch management, and he was generally well liked by the staff. Walter had Joel do an aptitude profile test on Stan and found him to be strongly dominant and quite analytical. He was short on empathy, and he tended to be somewhat distrustful of others. He was, however, very well balanced, results oriented, and naturally motivated to work hard. Walter knew that he could handle the job of running the branch, but because of the profile he was somewhat concerned about Stan's ability to nurture and maintain good relationships with his staff. He decided that Stan was the best candidate he had and that he would counsel him on leadership before he took over the branch and provide ongoing coaching as required. He liked Stan and wanted to give him a chance to be a manager before he retired. He had been a loyal employee of Joshua's, and Walter felt he deserved the opportunity. Walter also believed that aptitude profiles should only account for approximately thirty percent of the decision-making process in any hiring or promotion situation.

When Walter talked to him about leadership, Stan was very open and made it clear that he was a hands-on kind of leader who would roll up his sleeves and go to work in any area of the shop. It was evident that Stan believed in teamwork. He showed no signs of male chauvinism and appeared to have none of the other prejudices that can often get managers into trouble. Stan appeared to have a good grasp of management techniques and clearly wanted to make Walter proud of him. Walter was comfortable that he had made the right choice.

Stan's first few weeks went well. His staff of thirty-five appreciated his knowledge and experience in the business and enjoyed his obvious emotional strength and willingness to pitch in and help out virtually anyone in the shop. As time went on, though, they began to pull away from him. A phenomenon Walter could not have foretold began to emerge as Stan began to settle into his role. By the end of his first year on the job, twelve of Stan's original employees had quit. Reports that Walter received from his regional manager indicated that morale was at an all-time low and sales were beginning to suffer.

Walter called Stan to find out what the problem might be. Stan was very cooperative with Walter but could shed no light on the problem. He simply had no idea why people appeared not to like working for him. He was not negative with Walter and did not attempt to blame others. He also wanted to know what the problem was because replacing employees was a difficult and time consuming process for him. Faced with no other solution, Walter decided to do a 360 review of Stan. During that process a number of his staff would be sent a survey they would answer anonymously and send into a central administrator who would collate the results and score Stan in several areas of performance. Although Stan would know who would receive the surveys to complete, he would have no idea which employee said what or who provided any particular comment or score. The results would be conveyed to him on a general, overall basis after which Walter and his regional manager could work with him to improve areas in which he was deficient.

The survey results made it clear that Stan was everything Walter thought he was. Employees believed Stan was intelligent, knowledgeable, hard working and ethical. He was also not overtly rude or abusive. The two areas where he scored extremely low were leadership and communication.

The single question on the survey that led Walter to further investigation asked, "Is your manager a good leader?" Stan scored less than thirty percent in that area. Walter knew that a manager who scored over seventy percent in all areas except leadership must have an incredibly poor ability to communicate with his people. Stan was clearly leading by example, but his employees were still not buying into his leadership. After giving Stan the results of the survey, he let him know that he would be speaking with a number of employees on a one-on-one basis to find what the problem stemmed from.

Once he began talking to the staff, it did not take Walter long to sort out the problem. What he found out was that Stan was extremely negative with his employees. He constantly told them what they were doing wrong, but he never told them when they had done something right. His staff meetings consisted of an array of negative statistics and negative commentary. He encouraged his staff to speak up at staff meetings, but when they spoke Stan generally told them they were wrong or they did not understand the question. Eventually, they all stopped speaking up at meetings. That silence caused Stan to believe they didn't care about what he had to say, and that caused him to drive his negative reinforcement home even harder. It was clear that although Stan was not deliberately abusive, he believed that motivation had to come from fear of failure and that to drive performance it was necessary to indicate that current performance was simply not good enough. He never complimented any employee on any small or large success, and he never celebrated good results or hard work by the team. The only message the employees of Stan's Joshua's Tires shop remembered hearing was that they were not good enough.

Walter knew instinctively that when human beings are told repeatedly they don't measure up or they are not good enough, they will eventually give up. Defeat will set in and production will grind to a crawl. He also knew that when a manager constantly points out negative issues to his staff and never provides positive feedback or reinforcement, they will begin to avoid him. They will want to stay under the radar in order to avoid his scrutiny. Stan never let up on the drive for increased performance. When one goal was reached, he immediately began driving for an even higher one without first giving credit to his team for having reached the last one. Employees began to deliberately hold back to avoid reaching performance goals because they knew that as soon as they were successful, they would only be rewarded with more work. Stan Harper did not understand *positive passion.* Like so many managers, he believed that negative reinforcement was the path to success. As he was rapidly finding out, he was very wrong.

When Walter told Stan what he had heard, Stan did not appear to be surprised. What he was surprised at was that Walter appeared to be siding with the employees. He felt when *positive passion* was being explained to him, Walter must have no idea about management at all. In Stan's mind, if you molly-coddled employees, they would be spoiled and you would never get the best out of them. He actually believed that he had to continually set the bar beyond their reach so they would never stop trying to reach it. He listened patiently to Walter, but he was not hearing the message.

Walter left Stan's shop that day believing he had made a breakthrough. Stan had thanked him for his advice and promised to do better. However, as soon as Walter had left the premises, Stan went right back to focus on the negative as a management style. He vowed to himself to prove to Walter that his management methods were better. He redoubled his efforts and set his performance goals higher than they had ever been before. Within three months ten more employees had quit, and Walter had to make another trip to meet with Stan.

During this visit Stan was visibly agitated. He knew Walter would be displeased that he had replaced twenty-two staff members in fifteen months. Walter, although pleasant, was clearly disappointed and once again had to make a hard decision.

"Stan, I must tell you that I like you a lot on a personal level," Walter said with a smile. "However, our hiring and training costs in your branch are the highest in the company. In addition to that, the production here is almost thirty percent lower than it was when you took over fifteen months ago. I am afraid that I just cannot allow this to continue." He paused to allow Stan to speak.

"I know all that, Walter. What I can't figure out is why in heck these people won't listen to me. I work hard, I train them, I give them all the tools to be successful, and yet they continue to disappoint me. What am I doing wrong, Walter?" Stan asked pleadingly.

"Stan, it is clear to me that you didn't listen to a word I said the last time I was here. People are not horses. You can't beat them to make them run faster. You have to lead them, you have to reward them, and you have to show that you care. Your way might have worked during a time in history when there were more people than jobs and money was scarce. However, in this day and age you have to treat people like equals, and you have to tell them when they are doing well. You can't guilt them into working harder, and you can't motivate them with fear," Walter said confidently.

"So what now, Walter?" Stan asked calmly.

Walter sat back and thought for a moment before saying, "Well, now I would like you to go back to your job in the service shop. You were one of our best hands back there, and frankly, I think that is where you belong. Management just isn't right for you."

Stan responded almost immediately, "Okay, Walter. I'm good with that. I hate being in management anyway. Every time one of these people quit, I would take it as a personal failure, but I couldn't figure out what to do about it. I hope the next guy is better at it than me. These folks deserve better."

Walter felt good about his decision and was happy that Stan decided to stay on with Joshua's. However, he did not feel good about his decision to move Stan into management in the first place. He knew that it was an emotional decision on his part due to loyalty to Stan based on his long service. It is very common for leaders to make the mistake of advancing loyal employees to positions which they have no ability to handle as a reward for good work or friendship. Those decisions generally result in failure, and Walter would attempt to avoid similar situations in the future.

As Walter pondered the events of the past, he thought about how he had approached each one of them and how different each person and each situation was. "No two people are the same," he thought. Walter hated opera. The powerful voices of the tenors and baritones pouring out emotional songs in European languages did nothing for him. His mentor, Joshua O'Hare on the other hand, loved the genre and went to operatic performances every chance he got. That thought led Walter to the realization that all human beings are an audience unto themselves. Every person enjoys his or her own style of music, and each one them feels and thinks differently about every aspect of life. What we say and what we feel will not touch everyone in the same way. If we want to make a difference, we must either select an audience that instinctively and miraculously hears and understands what we say implicitly, or we must treat each person or each audience in a different way. We must always seek to touch a special chord in our audience. That chord must be in the key that touches the heartstrings of the listener. Our message may be the wrong one from time to time. Leaders who practice ***positive passion*** will accept that potential flaw and adjust their delivery in a tangible and effective way in order to make a positive impact on everyone they work with.

Walter's musings led him to think about some of the hard things he was forced to say to some of the people he had disciplined over the years. Despite the degree of difficulty, he knew those conversations were the most effective ones he could have. Leaders must have the courage to be honest when speaking to employees about their performance and attitude. If these employees don't know what they are doing wrong, they will never have an opportunity to improve. ***Good leaders sometimes have an opportunity to create good followers simply by pointing them in the right direction.*** Directionless employees, on the other hand, will simply spin out of control.

Walter's mind was racing now. He felt good and knew that he would be ready to give the presentation of his life at the spring leadership conference.

CHAPTER SEVEN

A *Positive Passion* Presentation

*When you speak from your heart
you open the door to your soul...*

CHAPTER 7

A *Positive Passion* Presentation

When Walter peered out onto the stage in the auditorium, he was taken aback by the number of people in the audience. Even though he had been responsible for much of the growth of Joshua's Tires, he seldom thought about just how many locations and how many managers they actually had. After Joshua O'Hare retired, Walter had grown the company to three hundred locations throughout North America with another three in Europe and four in Asia. "Jeez, there are a lot of people out there who will be staring at me!" he thought fleetingly. Walter knew it was natural to be nervous for the first few minutes of every public speaking event, but even with that knowledge he found himself trying to fight off feelings of fear at each presentation. To make things even more daunting, Joshua O'Hare had just given a rousing twenty-minute speech full of pride and optimism about the company he had started several years prior. The audience loved him, and there wasn't a dry eye in the house. Josh was a hard act to follow.

Although Walter had not given a lengthy presentation in several years, he was no stranger to public speaking. He was still a member of Toastmasters, and he made a point of giving a speech at the grand opening of every new Joshua's Tires shop. He knew that first impressions mattered tremendously in these situations. Although the content of a good speech will usually carry the day, if the speaker does not allow the audience to warm to him in the first few minutes, it is much harder to hold their attention. All public speakers know they should tell a joke or a personal story to warm things up. Walter knew that humor was risky because his sense of humor might not be the same as that of people in the audience. A bad or poorly received joke is much worse than no joke at all. A bad joke can actually turn the audience against the speaker, damaging his credibility and potentially harming the effectiveness of the entire presentation. He decided instead to follow Joshua's lead and talk about the success of the company. Today's audience represented the management team for his entire company, and he did not want to take a chance on offending even one of them.

Much to Walter's delight and surprise, when he walked out from behind the curtain onto the stage, he was greeted by immediate and deafening applause. The din of the clapping was accompanied by whistling and shouts of, "Go, Walter, Go!" He wasn't prepared for such an overwhelming response but it made him beam with pride. It was all he could do to remove the smile from his face as he moved his arms up and down in a motion intended to end the applause. When he finally brought the audience to order, he knew he had to say something great. Expectations were high and he didn't want to let them down.

"So, how are the best managers in the world feeling today?" Walter yelled into the microphone. That was met with another round of applause, whistling, and supportive shouting. That response was all the answer he needed. He knew at that moment that the audience was already warm to him and that a joke or a personal story would not be necessary.

When the applause died down, Walter said calmly and humbly, "Thank you so much for your kindness. I know that you are all busy people, and I know that you have better things to do than listen to me. I also know that you came here expecting to hear something good, and I hope I don't let you down. Firstly, let me tell you how proud I am of each and every one of you. The growth of our company over the past year has been phenomenal, and it is all because of you. It wasn't anything I did. It was each and every one of you who made Joshua's Tires one of the strongest companies in the world and by far the best place in the world to work." Again his comments were met with thunderous applause.

Walter could feel his confidence rising. The physiology of his body was changing. The natural symptoms of nervousness were beginning to ebb. His heart rate was slowing down to almost normal, he was beginning to perspire less, the salivary glands in his mouth were beginning to produce adequate amounts of saliva again, and his breathing was becoming normal so that he no longer felt as though he would run out of breath before he ended each sentence. He was in control and his body was telling him that all of his systems were normal. He knew that he would now be able to concentrate on the specific details of his presentation in relative physical and emotional comfort.

"On to business!" he shouted into the microphone. "I think you have all heard the expression *positive passion.* Some of you understand the implications of that concept and some of you don't. Firstly, let me tell you that I learned about *positive passion* from none other than Joshua O'Hare. Joshua never actually used those words, but he lived every day of his life with *positive passion* in his heart. You all heard him speaking a few minutes ago. Was he not the happiest, most buoyant and proud man you have every seen or heard in your life? Joshua lives for this company and it was his loyalty, his courage, his support, and his love of his employees that brought me here. Without Joshua O'Hare we would have nothing. I learned everything I know about management and leadership from him, and all I want now is to teach as much of it as I can to all of you."

Again, the applause began. Walter knew this applause was not for him. It was for Joshua, and that made him proud and happy.

"So what is **positive passion**?" he began again. He let the question dangle for a few seconds, just long enough for it to sink in. When Walter saw people beginning to lean over to their neighbors whispering, he knew they were beginning to think about his question. He didn't want an answer just yet, though, so he began speaking as soon as he spied a young man in the audience who appeared about to shout out an answer. It was not that Walter did not want audience participation. It was that he wanted to make his perspective clear and concise before he opened it up to questions. There is a fine line between an informational presentation and a seminar. Because of time limitations, Walter had decided to make this a presentation format. He simply could not put on a seminar with workshop-style interactive discussions, breakout groups or debates. The group was too large and his time was too short.

"I will not give you a one-liner explaining what **positive passion** is. Instead, I am going to give you a plan for leadership that will make your lives much easier. The big bonus is that when you master this principle, your branches will be even more profitable than they already are, and you will have more time to focus on managing that growth. Your current staffing challenges will be reduced and your ability to deal with difficult situations will be enhanced. **Positive passion** is about clarity and awareness. It is about understanding *people*. You already know everything there is to know about the tire business. You already have the hard skills: Inventory, Accounting, Marketing, Sales, Installation, Parts and Service. Those are the activities that we do, where we spend ninety percent of our time along with ninety percent of our training dollars. However, my friends, if we don't have happy, loyal, positive employees we won't grow and we won't maintain our position as the best employer in the business with the strongest balance sheet. If you don't know how to make a difference in the lives of your people, you will fail just as surely as an eagle that tries to fly with a broken wing. That majestic bird will not be able to get the lift it needs to take off because it simply cannot use all of its strength to move the air past its body. No matter how majestic the performance of your branch is today, the strength of your organization is in your employees, and if you don't have all of them giving you the positive lift that you need, you will come crashing to earth just as surely as that injured eagle every time it tries to take off." With that Walter took a deep breath and surveyed the audience. You could hear a pin drop as the Joshua's managers waited for Walter's next comment.

"So now let's take the term ***positive passion*** and try to understand why it has such great meaning for me. You all know what passion is. To me, it is an overwhelming feeling of desire and attraction for something or someone. When we are passionate, we are consumed by the object of our passion and every fiber of our being is dedicated to it. Passion actually creates pleasurable physical changes in our bodies as our endorphins take over. Human beings have passion for many things: their spouses, their cars, their favorite sport and even their jobs." On that comment, Walter strode over to the table that held an overhead projector and picked up the remote control that was waiting there for him. When he pushed the button, the first slide came up with only two bright white words on a stark field of dark blue: **POSITIVE**

PASSION. Walter looked up at the screen momentarily as if to assure himself that the slide was correct before walking toward the front edge of the stage. He felt the need to get closer to the audience in order to emphasize his next words.

"Given my explanation of what passion is, you might think the term *positive passion* is an example of poor use of the English language. After all, how could passion be anything but positive? Furthermore, how can the word *passion* be used in a phrase without a specific subject to apply it to? I don't care what my high school English teacher might think!" Walter stated confidently. "This is not a literature lesson. The fact of the matter is that I want you all to be positive in everything you do, and I want you to be passionate about your positivism. Make no mistake, people; nobody ever became successful by being negative. Negative energy is wasted energy. If you remember only one thing from today, remember this: **Choose to be positive. Choose Success!** Remember, too, that without *positive passion* in your life, you will never progress from ordinary to spectacular or from mediocre to great. Positive energy is easy on the mind and kind to the soul. It makes you feel good and it makes your life better. Negative energy is abrasive and exhausting. Nothing good can come from it, and it can turn your life into a fragile shell shrouded in misery."

Walter needed to take a deep breath in order to carry on, so he used the opportunity to turn toward the screen behind him and advance the projector to the next slide. As he pushed the button on the remote control, a new slide appeared. All it contained was the word **POSITIVE** arranged vertically.

P
O
S
I
T
I
V
E

Walter turned to his audience and walked toward the edge of the stage again. "So there you have it. That one word is the singular topic of my entire presentation today. Keep looking at it while I talk to you a little bit. You will find in the course of your business and personal lives that there are plenty of times when you would like to choose negativity. Some of the things that lead to that choice include employees who come in late, employees who make too many personal phone calls, habitual underperformers, and children who don't do their homework. Faced with those challenges you might choose anger, disappointment, depression, or frustration as your emotions. All of them are negative. You might choose yelling, cursing, criticizing, accusing or the silent treatment as actions. All are negative responses to an already unpleasant situation. Your emotions combined with your actions will take something as small and insignificant as a personal phone call and turn it into a life-changing event for both you and your victim. I use the word *victim* because the person on the receiving end of those negative actions and emotions will feel very much like a victim, and they will not believe for one second that they deserve the treatment you are dishing out. When that happens, all normal human communication will come to an end, and while you are reacting to their negative behavior, they will be accusing you of unfair and inappropriate negative discipline.

Where I come from, two negatives don't make a positive; they just make a bigger negative. Your victims might internalize their disgust for your actions, or they might fight back. Either way, you will have lost. Any opportunity you might have had to convince them of the error of their ways and assist them in doing better will be lost. You see, folks, negativity creates negativity. It has a single purpose. It can't escape from itself and create anything good. It can only continue to spread unhappiness wherever it goes. If you eliminate negative thoughts and actions from your life, things will immediately improve for you. Trust me, ***positive passion*** is the only way to go if you want to be successful and happy." Walter stopped speaking and stared out into the sea of silent faces. Wanting to bring them back from their thoughts of their own negative actions in the past, he said in a loud voice, "So, who wants to be happy?" A weak murmur of laughter emerged from the floor.

"I will ask you again! Who in this room wants to be happy?!!!" Walter yelled at the top of his lungs while raising his hands high over his head.

"WE DO!!!" came the thunderous response from the Joshua's managers. It was followed by joyful laughter and happy chatter from every corner of the room. Walter knew then that he had captured their hearts and souls and that he had their full attention. Grabbing the moment, he pushed the remote control button to bring up the next slide. Suddenly a group of letters flew in from the left of the slide, and the **E** in the word **POSITIVE** became the word **EXCITEMENT**.

P
O
S
I
T
I
V
EXCITEMENT

The murmur and laughter emanating from the crowd came to an end as they looked toward the screen, wondering what Walter was going to say next.

"I have created an anagram to help you remember *positive passion* and the value of it. Each letter of the word **POSITIVE** will relate to a word that will help emphasize the significance of always being positive. Starting at the bottom and working to the top, I have chosen *excitement* to represent the *E*. One of the most important things about *positive passion* is the excitement it can bring to you and every one around you. Of course, you will not find excitement until you make the commitment to bring passion to everything you do, and bring it in a consistently positive way.

When you are dealing with people at work or elsewhere, always show them that you are excited about your work. You must always lead by example, and remember that as leaders, you are on stage twenty-four hours a day, seven days a week. If you are not excited about your work, others will sense it. When that happens, it will send a message to your employees that your work is not important to you. If your work seems unimportant, they will feel that their work is even less important.

You must also show excitement about the work your employees do. Catch them *doing things right* and be enthusiastic about their accomplishments. Put them on a pedestal and celebrate their successes. A cautionary note about celebrating: never make the mistake of taking credit for an employee's accomplishments or giving more credit to our company than to your workers. Understand, too, that you must always make sure their co-workers know that you have congratulated them for a job well done. If it is a private celebration between you and one employee, there will be no broad-ranging effect. Put their names up in lights for all to see. Everyone likes a pat on the back, and when the others see it happening, they will strive to be next on your appreciation list. You already have the top job in your branch, and our company certainly doesn't need any kudos, so make it all about them. If you are excited about your employees, they will be excited about you. If they are excited about you, they will do their best every day, and ultimately your job will become easier and your branch will be more profitable.

You must also be excited about your job and our company when you are dealing with clients and people you meet socially. After all, if the manager is down on Joshua's Tires, why would anyone else want to deal with us? If the manager doesn't like his or her job at Joshua's Tires, why would anyone want to come to work for us? This is extremely important. You are the official representatives of our company in your communities, and all eyes are on you. It is how you conduct yourself and how much enthusiasm and excitement you show for our firm that will make the difference between success and failure in your branches.

Now, I don't want to scare anyone off with this last comment about excitement, but I have to say that if you are not excited about your job in our company - if you don't have the passion - you need to take a long, hard look at yourself and decide if this is the career for you. I often find that if the excitement is not there, people will *quit and stay*. If you find yourself not wanting to get out of bed and come to work at Joshua's every morning, you might be in the wrong job, and you might have quit and stayed. When that happens you will be no good for your staff, you will be no good for our company, you will be no good for your families, and frankly, you will be no good for yourself." Walter stopped speaking and took a big drink of water from the glass that was on the table that held the overhead projector. He knew that his last comments would start people thinking, and he wanted to give the gravity of his words time to sink in.

At this point in the proceedings, no one in the audience was speaking, whispering or smiling. They were concentrating on Walter and they wanted to hear more. Feeling the energy of the crowd, Walter pushed the remote control button again. This time a group of letters came cartwheeling in from the right. The **V** in **POSITIVE** magically became the word **VISION**.

P
O
S
I
T
I
VISION
EXCITEMENT

Walter looked out at the audience and smiled as he began speaking. "So who here has a vision for the future?" he asked in a loud voice. For a moment all he could see were smiles in the audience, but gradually he saw people leaning over to each other to discuss his question.

Suddenly a young man in the front row cupped his hands around his mouth and yelled out, "You do, Walter!"

"Ha, ha, ha!" Walter laughed genuinely. "Good answer, Mark! However, it is tremendously important not only that I have vision, but that each and every one of you has it as well. Let's remember that this session is about ***positive passion.*** The vision I want you all to adopt is a vision for fairness, compassion, and personal growth for you and for everyone you work with. When you wake up in the morning, you need to clear your mind of negative thoughts and choose to have a great day. Each day, your vision should be of positive events. If you visualize only positive things, you will quite naturally encounter more positive events than negative ones. If you wake up and consciously assume that bad things are going to happen, you will almost always realize that vision. You generate your own energy and you create your own reality. Think positive and *be* positive.

In your branches you must have a vision for the future of the business and it must include each and every person there. Remember that just as you had ambition to be managers, each of your employees has ambition for themselves. You must find out what their vision for their future is and assist them in attaining it. If they don't believe that your vision of your branch includes them in any significant way, you will lose them. You have to get beyond your own vision and think about the visions of everyone around you. That is *real* vision, people!

Also, folks, I want you to think beyond the corporate memos and procedural manuals that you have on your credenzas. If something is good for your employees and is not illegal or fabulously expensive, do it! Take charge of your branch and run it like you own it. Create a vision for your branch. I only ask that you use common sense and always include your employees in decisions whenever you can. You might think I am being cavalier or a little reckless right now, but believe me when I say that every manager we have ever had that has stepped out and managed his or her branch as though they owned it has made me proud. Take a chance. And always remember that you have several good brains with great visions of their own at your personal disposal every day. Those brains belong to your employees, folks, and they can make you or break you depending on how you deal with them. Utilize them in a positive fashion and you will win." With that, Walter paused and surveyed the crowd.

"So who has vision now?" he yelled.

"I do!" yelled Mark from the front row. His exuberance was met with laughter and applause from the audience. Mark Peters was a popular young manager of a Joshua's shop in Oregon. He ran a very successful branch but was most well known for his wonderful sense of humor and his unabashed desire to be the center of attention in any setting. Walter liked him and appreciated his participation in his presentation.

Walter shook his finger at Mark and shot him a big smile before pushing the remote control button again. He couldn't have been happier at this moment. His presentation was going over well, the audience was happy, and he was completely relaxed. This was how he had visualized it while he was writing his initial notes, and he was quite proud that he was carrying it off. The next push of the button had another group of letters tumbling in from the top this time. The **I** in **POSITIVE** was transformed into the word **INTEREST**.

P
O
S
I
T
INTEREST
VISION
EXCITEMENT

Walter put the microphone right up against his chin to enhance the effect of what he was about to say next. "I am interested in all of you," he said softly but sincerely. The microphone picked up the quieter tone of his voice and amplified it which gave it a hollow, almost eerie tone. Raising his voice suddenly he said, "In fact I want to get to know everything I can about each and everyone of you. I want to know about your homes, your families, your hopes, your dreams, your desires, and anything else I can find out about you. I want you to follow your hearts and I want to help you reach your goals. I am not in this business because I have an overwhelming interest in tires. I am in this business because I am interested in you!" Walter pulled the microphone away from his face and surveyed the crowd. "How many of you can say that you feel the same way about each and every employee in your branch?" he challenged.

The audience members were silent again. Some smiled knowingly, some were stone-faced and some looked embarrassed. Each person knew exactly what Walter was asking, and each person was mentally reviewing their relationships with their own employees.

"If you don't feel the same way I do, then you had better start!" he continued. "There is an old adage that says the more you tell people about yourself, the more they will like you. The reason for that is by exposing your innermost thoughts, feelings and vulnerabilities to them, you build trust. If you do not create trust with your people, you will never get their respect and they will never give you their best. Once they trust you, they will begin to tell you about themselves. They will want to talk to you about their problems, their hopes, their dreams and their desires. When you show that you are interested in them and really listen to what they have to say, they will want to tell you more. Knowledge is power, folks, and the more you know about your employees, the more you can inspire them to give.

By the way, don't make the mistake of always talking about yourself, and never brag about the things you have done or are planning to do. Tell them factually and without embellishment about your family your home, or your career. Show your vulnerability and let them know that you have problems too. Let them know that you are not always right and that you have made mistakes. In short, *be human*. You will never gain the trust of your employees with a superior attitude or by lording your success or status over them. Speak at their level with humility and candor.

Once you have their trust, draw them out and show a great deal of interest in the things they say. Let them know that you care about their kids and that you want them to enjoy their time with their spouses and friends. When one of them comes back from a vacation, don't immediately tell them that work has piled up while they were gone or give them a list of problems they need to deal with. Ask them first how the vacation went and show genuine interest in whatever details they want to give you. Once they have bonded with you at that level, they will much more readily accept the reality of what you have to tell them about their job. And by the way, don't make them feel bad about going on vacation. I see that happening every day. Yes, it is inconvenient when we are short staffed due to vacation, but every human being needs time off to recharge their batteries, and it is up to you make sure, firstly, that your people take their vacations and, secondly, that they feel good about the time off. If they are stressed out about being away from work the whole time, the vacation will do them no good at all.

Show your interest in their work, too. Ask them how they are doing. Occasionally ask if you can assist and then roll up your sleeves and help them do their job if they respond in the affirmative. Again, catch people doing things right and reward them. Every time you show any amount of interest in the work of your employees, you will gain strength with them, and mark my word, folks, your job will be easier.

Now, this is so important: always show interest your own work, too. Talk about what you do in the course of your day and speak positively about it. Set the example for enthusiasm on the job. Never betray confidences or release confidential information, but do talk positively about your employees and give examples of people who are doing great work. Talk about the future of the business and how your people can contribute to the success of it during the coming months and years.

Tell your people what you like about your job and how you would like to improve things. Ask for their advice and let them know their opinions matter. Every one of your people has at least one good idea. If you use one of them, let everyone know whose idea it was and consider a reward program for ideas that make money or save money for the branch.

The bottom line is that if you show interest in your people, you will improve the performance of your business. With consistent interest your profits will soar and your job will be a piece of cake!"

Walter surveyed the crowd and noticed they were nodding in approval and whispering to each other. He could tell he had covered the subject well enough and had their agreement. He pushed the button on his remote to reveal the next word. The **T** in **POSITIVE** was suddenly joined by several more letters that spelled the word **TOLERANCE**.

P
O
S
I
TOLERANCE
INTEREST
VISION
EXCITEMENT

"This might be the most important element of all when we are talking about *positive passion*, folks!" Walter stated with conviction. "You must all learn to be tolerant of many things. No two people are the same, and each one brings his or her own set of good and bad characteristics. You have to allow them to co-exist and understand that nobody is capable of pleasing all of the people all of the time." Walter had not taken a drink of water for quite some time, and he could feel the inside of his lips beginning to stick to his teeth as he spoke. He excused himself and took a big tug of water from his glass before continuing.

When he was refreshed, Walter's face took on a serious look as he said, "Let me cover the obvious areas where we must all be tolerant just in case there is anyone here that that doesn't know them. You must never be intolerant of any particular race, creed or color. This is the twenty-first century, and frankly, I insist that anyone working for me is completely free of petty, Neanderthal prejudices. Racial tolerance is not really tolerance at all. What right does any human being have to *tolerate* or *not tolerate* the existence of another human being? Racial tolerance is simple acceptance of all mankind, and it is the only way to live our lives at work and at home."

You must always be tolerant of the opposite sex as well. This is commonly a problem for men. We still have a few male chauvinists in our company who don't seem to understand that women have the right to work and succeed in the same positions as men, and we have no right to stand in their way. If anyone here doesn't understand that, then come and see me after the session so that I can explain it to you. And ladies, you are not all completely innocent either. I have heard some serious examples of man-bashing over the years, and I am here to tell you that it is no more acceptable than male chauvinism. If you want to be respected in the workplace, then you need to understand there must be no gender barriers or discrimination of any kind from either gender!" That comment brought some gasps and giggles from the crowd, and Walter knew that it might even have offended some of the women. However, he knew he had gotten the point across and was confident that he was right in saying it.

"The next thing on my list is religion," Walter said calmly. "We must respect the religion of everyone who works for us, and we have no right to prevent anyone from practicing it. It is not something that should be actively practiced in the workplace, but we should make every effort to accommodate our various cultures and never make negative or defamatory remarks.

The big one that encompasses a large segment of society is tolerance of minorities. There are a myriad of minorities in our society, and we simply must be *bigger* people, not *bigot* people. Let's be known as the company that celebrates the differences of every segment of society and the one that employs as many minorities as we can!" Walter moved the microphone away from his face at that moment in order to allow the last comment to sink in.

Much to his surprise, everyone in the audience sprang up at once, clapping hands in a thunderous standing ovation. He knew then that he and his executive team had chosen wisely when they hired this group of managers and he was proud. He took another drink of water as he held back the tears of joy and pride welling up in his eyes. After a few seconds, he walked to the edge of the stage and motioned for the group to sit down so he could continue speaking.

"Thanks for that, my friends. You have no idea how much your support means to me," he said softly and sincerely. "But now, I want to talk about some other areas of intolerance. We have to accept the fact that some people laugh differently or more loudly than others. We have to accept that some of our staff come from different socio-economic backgrounds than others, and we have to accept that some of our people are simply smarter than others. Some folks speak with an accent and some are fat. Some are tall and some walk with a limp. They say that it takes all kinds to make a world, and if we are going to grow and prosper, we are going to hire people of all different kinds. Each person that we employ will have a different skill level than all others, and each person will perform better in one job than another. Every single person we have chosen to hire and bring into our Joshua's family must be treated with the same level of respect. It is up to us as managers to put the right people into the right jobs and then support them. If we find negative behavior among employees, we must deal with it head on and let our other employees know that discriminatory behavior is simply not allowed in our corporate culture.

Don't forget about the little things either. Some people have a habit of cracking their knuckles, some chew too loud, and some may have bad body odor. And how about that incredibly annoying habit of being too cheerful? Remember that being annoying is not grounds for termination. I expect none of you to overreact to these situations, and I also expect you to coach your staff to be more tolerant. Often when someone has an annoying habit, all it takes is a kind word to the individual mentioning that it is a problem. No one wants to be annoying, after all, and generally someone who is aware will do everything possible to avoid the habit. However, left unchecked these situations can cause rumors, gossip, general bad behavior throughout the employee group, and ultimately someone might get hurt. If you nip these things in the bud, you will save yourself a lot of grief in the long run.

You, my friends, must be the bastions of fair play and tolerance for our company. You must be the leaders who guide your people to a kinder, better work day. This is a very special area of management, and I am here to tell you that if you can perfect it, you will find yourself working with the happiest, most well adjusted team in the world. Be the best you can be and others will follow!" As he finished his thought, Walter noticed the people in the audience were nodding, smiling, and making sounds of acceptance. They felt the power of *positive passion*, and he knew it.

Feeling he had covered the last subject adequately, Walter pushed the remote button and watched as the next **I** in the word **POSITIVE** was magically transformed into the word **INTELLIGENCE**.

```
          P
          O
          S
    INTELLIGENCE
      TOLERANCE
       INTEREST
        VISION
      EXCITEMENT
```

"Whoa, Betsy! I bet you are all hoping that I am not about to tell you that you are not intelligent. Well, I'm not!" Walter said with a laugh. "However, I am going to tell you that you probably don't use your intelligence at all times."

Walter knew there is huge value in shocking the audience to attention. By telling them that they do not use their intelligence, he sparked their interest and focused their attention on what he was about to say next. He knew that long, boring speeches that just spew out a large number of facts and figures are not memorable at all. They are really just a waste of everyone's time. It is important to break up the material with laughs, shock value, and psychological curve balls. He also knew that it was important not to stand in one spot while speaking. He refused to use a lectern and moved around the stage constantly. Audience members need to see movement and hear a variety of tones and thoughts if they are going to remain focused for the full duration of the presentation. Walter's rule of thumb was that he would not stand in one spot longer than two to three minutes. In his early days of public speaking he actually experimented with these techniques, and once while speaking, he deliberately did not move from one spot for fifteen minutes. What he found was that not only was the audience almost completely expressionless, but after about ten minutes they became fidgety and started having conversations among themselves. They were so bored by his delivery that they became completely disengaged from his presentation. When he finally moved energetically across the stage, he noticed that the eyes of the audience returned to him, and they began to show emotional responses to his words again. It was as though he had flipped a switch in their brains.

"So let's talk about intelligence as it relates to ***positive passion,***" he said sincerely. "There are two types of intelligence: the kind that resides in your brains and allows you to function, and the kind the CIA has. As you all know, the Central Intelligence Agency is not an organization dedicated to the development and nurturing of intelligent people." That comment brought a rumble of laughter from the crowd. Walter chose not to dwell on the potentially humorous element of that statement and moved on.

He made a gesture with his arms to stop the laughter, and when he had regained control he said, "The CIA is dedicated to gathering information that will allow them to anticipate criminal activity and protect the United States from threats by other countries or from within. Hence the intelligence they speak of has little to do with intellect. It is instead valuable information that allows them to do their job of protecting American citizens on all fronts. You need the same kind of intelligence the CIA has if you are going to be effective in your job of leading your staff and protecting the interests of Joshua's Tires." Walter could see the audience was becoming confused by his analogy as they squirmed about in their seats and whispered to their neighbors. He was enjoying the intrigue that he had created.

"What I am saying is that you must know what you are doing, and you must know what you are talking about, folks!" he said loudly. "When you are disappointed in one of your employees, you need to know exactly what they are doing wrong, why they are doing it wrong and how you can correct the problem. There is no point in disciplining people if you don't know why they are exhibiting the behavior that is upsetting you. For example, if someone comes in late, do you always know what is going on at home? Do you know what the situation is with their health? Do you know if they are having financial difficulties and can't afford to drive? Do you know if they have moved to a new home and haven't synchronized their timing yet? Rather than flying off the handle and making a mountain out of a molehill, you need to find out what is going on. That is a minor example, but I have more.

I once had a salesman out in Vancouver who had quite severe Attention Deficit Hyperactive Disorder. His manager was totally frustrated with him because his attitude around the office was deplorable. He was a great salesman and always hit all of his sales targets, but he was so toxic around the branch that no one wanted to have anything to do with him. The manager had no understanding about his ADHD and just thought the guy was a trouble maker. He was seriously considering termination, but after he spoke with me and I filled him in on the problems the fellow had, he came up with a scheme to help him fit in. Armed with the intelligence he needed, the manager was able to make an almost complete turnaround in the salesman, and he is still generating top sales results to this very day. He has also become a model employee, and his co-workers love having him around. Had the manager not taken the time to seek out help and get the information he needed, we might very well have lost a very good employee.

One of the most tragic scenarios I have ever had to deal with was with a manager who almost made it to the top of the ladder while leaving a trail of destruction behind him. When he made it to Regional Vice

President of Sales, his negative behavior finally hit the radar. A few people had resigned from our company while working for him, and nobody thought too much of it. However, when three of our top managers gave their notice on the same day, citing this man as the reason, I realized he was a major threat to our operation and I had to do something. The fact is that I was to blame in that situation because I had never taken the time to profile him. It became clear over time that this fellow was not at all capable of managing people, and frankly, could not manage himself. He could not lead others because he never learned to lead himself. He was operating in a sphere of negativity that had completely consumed him. When I finally got around to damage control for the problems he had created, I decided to have an aptitude profile done on him. It was glaringly clear that he suffered from chronic self loathing and had virtually no empathy for others. Here is where the *positive passion* comes in, folks; I did not fire him. Instead I recognized that I set him up for failure, and I chose to right that wrong by helping him find a better path. He still works for us and is doing quite well. It was lack of intelligence on my part that allowed him to fail. When I finally got the intelligence I needed, I was able to see beyond the symptoms of his problems to find the root cause.

You are all experts in the tire business. That is because we give you intelligence about tires, brakes and valve stems. You know what our competitors are charging for their products, and you know what market segments are the best for us to attack with sales campaigns. Like the CIA, you are constantly doing research and seeking out intelligence to stay one step ahead. You have intelligence in accounting, and you have intelligence in marketing and stock ordering. What you do not have is intelligence about your employees. You spend all your time learning the nuts and bolts of our business, but you seldom spend even five minutes finding out about what makes your people think what they are thinking or why they perform the way they do.

And don't forget to look for intelligence about yourself, too. If someone on you staff doesn't trust you or is upset with you for some reason, they will not do good work for you. If you find someone doing less than acceptable work or giving you the cold shoulder, ask them what is wrong. Have the courage to find out if *you* are the problem. You can't fix what you don't know, so simply ask them what you can do to improve. If you provide them with a safe, unthreatening environment and listen to what they have to say, you just might learn something. You might get some intelligence!

I cannot emphasize enough that your team is your strength, and you need to find out everything you can about them. Make sure you do your research on your people so that you can keep them happy and put the right people into the right jobs. You can't help them become better if you don't know anything about them. That my friends, is real intelligence!" Walter's voice was loud and resounded through the public address system as he spoke those last words. He was a natural master of emphasis and microphone technique. His presentation style had everyone in the room on the edge of their seats.

"I know you are all intelligent, so all you need now is some real intelligence!" he said with a laugh while pushing the button on his remote control. This time a jumble of letters flew around the screen before landing beside the **S** in **POSITIVE**. The word they spelled was **SENSITIVITY**.

P
O
SENSITIVITY
INTELLIGENCE
TOLERANCE
INTEREST
VISION
EXCITEMENT

"My friends, I hope you all pay close attention to this section of my presentation," Walter said sincerely. "***Positive passion*** is all about sensitivity. It is about being sensitive to people. If you are not capable of opening up your hearts and minds in order to understand the people in your lives, you will never be successful. Sensitivity is something that comes naturally to people who have powerful social values but not so naturally to people who do not have a highly developed sense of empathy for others. I am not talking about sending people home when they are not feeling well, or giving time off for traumatic or emotional personal events. I think it's great when any of you shown concern for someone who has had a death in the family or when you send flowers to someone who has had a baby. However, everyone is capable of those obvious displays of sensitivity. What I am talking about is being sensitive enough to be able to *read* people and allow them to be themselves while they are at work.

When you are empathetic, you put yourself in the shoes of another person in order to make a serious effort to understand what their motivations are and what they are feeling. Then and only then can you influence them to begin thinking your way. As managers we often have an inclination to simply *tell* our employees what they need to do and how to do it. When we operate in that fashion, we are often disappointed by their performance and end up scratching our heads, wondering what is wrong with *them. They* are not the problem! The problem is usually that *you* have not motivated them! You have not touched a chord in them that provides them with a desire to do their work and do it well." Walter stopped speaking for a moment in order to take a sip of water. That also gave him a chance to glance about the crowd in order to gauge their reactions. He was happy with what he was saying and confident that his team was giving it serious thought.

"So how do I become more sensitive? Is that what you are thinking?" he asked to nods and interrogative grunts from the audience. "Firstly, you need to slow down. You need to realize that your people need time to mentally process the things you say to them. They need to understand what you are asking of them, and then they need to be allowed to let their own minds frame it in such a way that it not only makes sense to them but feels good to them. They need the time to massage the information so it becomes something they can identify with based on their own motivators and behaviors.

Once they accept that you have provided them with a great idea and allowed them to find a way to get the job done that works for them, they will start working conscientiously. If they think you are just giving them another *order*, they will procrastinate and plod through the work, resentful of it and of you! Have the sensitivity to slow down and let your people think for themselves. Tell them what needs to be done, but let them decide on the method they will use to get it done. Once your people have passed the trainee stage, they no longer need to be guided, instructed or ordered to do anything. Have the sensitivity to let them think for themselves, then open yourself up enough to be available and approachable for any questions or assistance that may be required. Human beings are not machines, and Joshua's Tires is not the Marine Corps. Your employees need to be allowed to utilize their personal talents, skills and emotions in everything they do.

You should also learn to be sensitive to their body language and facial expressions in order to determine if they are onside with you and understanding you. Scowling, frowning, twitching or inappropriate smiling are obvious signs of disagreement. However, folks, when you are speaking with an employee, you need to look into their eyes for more subtle indications. Look for signs of squinting, eye rolling, looking down or looking from side to side. All may be signs of rejection of what the person is hearing from you. The eyes are the window to the soul, and you need to be able to read them. When someone is getting what you are saying and agreeing with it, their eyes will probably be sparkling bright and looking squarely into yours.

Body language is tough to read, but it is important to pay attention to it. If someone is squirming around in their chair, slouching, looking up at the ceiling, flicking lint from the their pants or doing anything other than sitting up and looking at your face while you are speaking, they are probably not really listening to you.

If you sense from what you are seeing in the person that they are disagreeing with you or rejecting your comments altogether, you need to stop and ask them if they understand and agree. If they don't agree or understand, have the sensitivity to accept that for what it is and hear them out. It may simply be that you have to rephrase what you are saying or allow them to have some input so that whatever the subject may be, it is at least partly their idea.

You can't get anywhere with your people unless you are sensitive to their needs, wants, wishes, and motivations. You have to be a big enough person to understand that hardly anyone in your employ will agree with everything you say. The only way you can get the best from them is to be sensitive enough to accept that every person is an individual, and everyone will approach challenges in a different way.

Finally, folks, you need to be sensitive to your own actions. You need to understand that because you are on stage 24/7, your actions and attitudes are being watched by everyone at all times. In order to lead others, you must come to grips with your own behaviors and learn to conduct yourself in a manner that is beyond reproach. The old adage, "Put your mind in gear before you engage your mouth," is one that you all should live by. Remember that you are all individuals and no one else thinks like you. Again, I have to say that you will *not* get unconditional respect or agreement every time you speak. You will have to earn respect every day, and you will probably never get complete agreement from everyone. Learn to live with those realities and be diligent in your resolve while remaining the most sensitive leader you can be. If you fail to engage your employees, it is not their fault. It is yours and yours alone!" With that final statement on the subject of sensitivity, Walter moved the microphone away from his mouth and looked out into the voluminous room before him. His audience was silent and pensive. He knew that was a good sign.

Feeling it was time to move on, Walter pushed the button on his remote control to bring up the next word. This time a group of letters came flying in diagonally from the top, ending up in front of the letter **O** spelling the word **OPPORUNITY**.

P
OPPORTUNITY
SENSITIVITY
INTELLIGENCE
TOLERANCE
INTEREST
VISION
EXCITEMENT

"Second to last word, folks. Let's make it good!" Walter began. "What can I say about opportunity? I can say that *positive passion* is the best opportunity you will ever have for self improvement, self satisfaction, and happiness! If you practice what I have discussed with you today and live your life in a truly positive way, you will soon be happier, and you will sleep better at night. This is your opportunity for success in everything you do if you choose to utilize it.

Positive passion is an opportunity to grow as a person and to improve your relationships with virtually every person you come into contact with. Just think how much stress you could shed if you drove all negativity from your mind. The majority of stress we carry around with us is based in negative thoughts and negative situations. If you can simply begin to see only the positive elements of any situation and look for ways to be positive with every person you meet, you will find that stress will become a thing of the past, and you will greet every morning with a smile on your face. When you think negative thoughts you almost always create a negative result. If, for example, you believe that you are going to have a bad day, you will have a bad day…guaranteed! If you believe that one of your employees is going to let you down, they will surely let you down. If you believed this morning that you were not going to enjoy my presentation, then you are sitting there right now with a frown on your face, aren't you?" Walter's last question was a challenge to the crowd. After asking it, he put his hand to his forehead and moved his head back and forth as though he was looking for a person with a frown. All he found were big smiles and occasional laughter.

"Have you ever noticed who the popular men and women are in any group of people?" Walter asked. "They are generally the ones who have only good things to say about people, things, and situations. They constantly make positive comments and find the good in everyone. When someone does something good or bad, the popular people encourage them and offer them positive reinforcement. If something goes well, they pat them on the back. When something goes badly, they let them know that they have done their best and that they should keep trying. They turn every challenge into an opportunity to reinforce the value of each human being they meet.

Have you ever noticed which people are referred to as *nice* and which people are most trusted in any group of people? I have! They are those positive people who say kind, supportive things about everyone they meet. They never speak badly about anyone behind their backs, and they always counter negative commentary from others with a positive point of view. The thing I find interesting about this phenomenon is that mankind cherishes and reveres positive people, and yet most of us spend a huge amount of our time being negative. It is almost as if we choose to be negative because we think that a purely positive attitude is something we can never really achieve. We seem to feel that negativity is somehow honorable and appropriate when we are not getting our own way. We also seem to think negativity will somehow or other create a positive result. We think that if we criticize someone, they will become better. But they won't. We think that if we complain about a problem it will go away. But it won't. We think that if we speak badly about the place we work, our boss will find out about it and suddenly go out of his way to make things better for us. But I won't!" Walter finished with a laugh.

The audience laughed politely at Walter's last comment and then went silent, clearly thinking about their own negativity. Seeing their concentration, Walter was compelled to carry on.

"Your opportunity today is to hear my words and believe that you can live a positive, successful lifestyle. I used the word *successful* very deliberately just now. You will not become successful by being negative. Nothing good ever comes from negativity, so it follows that success is the natural byproduct of a positive attitude. Here are some examples you might want to consider if you want to improve your life: Never speak or think badly of your employees and peers. Never find fault with anything that is not abhorrently wrong or fundamentally flawed. Never use negative terminology when describing our products or services to clients or acquaintances. Never use sarcasm to make a statement about something or someone you don't approve of. Never offer a critical evaluation of anything without also offering a positive remedy for the problem. Finally, don't be a whiner or complainer, because frankly, no one likes those. I could go on all day, but I think you get my drift," Walter said in a kindly tone.

"This is your opportunity if you choose to accept it, folks! Choose to be positive. Choose to be happy and successful! Take the opportunity to be positive about every aspect of your life and you will always win. If you consistently offer positive reinforcement and positive energy to your employees, friends and loved ones, you will always be happy at home and at work. And that's how I really feel on the subject!" Walter said with true passion in his voice.

The next push of the remote control button brought a jumble of letters rolling and tumbling toward the last letter on the screen. The **P** in **POSITIVE** was suddenly transformed into the word **POWER**.

POWER

OPPORTUNITY

SENSITIVITY

INTELLIGENCE

TOLERANCE

INTEREST

VISION

EXCITEMENT

"This is it, folks!" Walter yelled into the microphone. "This is what we all came for! I am here today to tell you that I believe in *positive passion* because it is the most powerful thing in the world!

If you practice *positive passion*, you will have the power to accomplish anything and everything you want. Remember what I always say, "No one has ever succeeded through pure negativity." You cannot possibly get the things you want out of life unless you approach everything you do with a positive attitude. I want every one of you to be successful and I want every one of you to be the best you can be. Most importantly, though, I want every one of you to be happy. Happy people are the winners in our society, and they have the power to do anything they want!

The power of **_positive passion_** will make your job much easier, too. Imagine a workplace where everyone is happy! Imagine a workplace where every task that each and every one of your employees undertakes is done with a smile. Imagine how a consistently happy employee group could impact your sales. Just imagine the comments you would receive from your customers if they met nothing but happy, cheerful employees in every area of our Joshua's shops. Think about how easy your job would be if all your employees came to work with a good attitude every day, and none of them ever got into a dispute. Imagine what life would be like if none of your people ever talked badly about any of the others. How does that sound to you?" Walter stopped speaking and scanned the audience. Suddenly a shout came from the front row.

"That sounds pretty darned good to me, Walter!" yelled the ever faithful Mark Peters.

"Sounds good to me too!" yelled Jim Balderson from a table near the back of the room that Walter could barely see. Jim's support of Mark's outburst started the whole room shouting words of support, laughing and applauding. Finally everyone stood up and Walter received his second standing ovation of the day. He beamed with pride at the sheer magnificence of his team. As he fought back his tears, he realized that his managers loved him and he loved them back. The emotion of the moment was almost too much for him. After a respectful period of time, he motioned everyone to sit down so he could continue.

Walter walked to the very edge of the stage with his head down. He looked up and moved his eyes back and forth, surveying his team for a moment before speaking. The audience was totally silent as they waited for his next words. **"It all starts with you,"** he said in a whisper with the microphone pressed to his lips. The microphone picked up his words and the public address system amplified them through its huge speakers causing his message to echo in every corner of the room. The effect was exactly what Walter wanted.

"If you want to make yours the best shop in the Joshua's family, then remember what I have said to you today!" he said loudly. "I have something to help you. Have a look at this," he said as he pushed the button on his remote control again. The **POSITIVE** anagram disappeared from the screen and was instantaneously replaced by a chart that no one in the room would soon forget. The final piece of Walter's puzzle was **SUCCESS** and it was prominently displayed at the top of the chart.

"There you have it, folks. *Positive passion* equals success. I call these the *power boxes*. The box at the bottom where it all starts contains *positive passion*. If you live with **excitement, vision, interest, tolerance, intelligence, sensitivity, and take advantage of the opportunities** they bring, you will find the *power* that leads to *success*!" Walter said with confidence.

 "I don't think I have ever met a single human being who did not desire some form of success, so I thought you might be interested in this," Walter said with a smile. "I want you all to take this information back to your branches next week, and with that in mind, Joel has made up a kit with a pamphlet in it that will help you deliver this information to your employees. I want you all to hold staff meetings that are dedicated to the concept of *positive passion* as soon as possible. I want the concept to become part of the fabric of our culture here at Joshua's, and I want every employee to practice it. You will find that the pamphlet contains most of the information I have given you so far today, and it also contains some examples of things not to do. I didn't want to give you the kit before I spoke because I knew that you would all be reading it instead of listening to me. And you know how I like to be the center of attention," he said with a laugh.

"So that's about it for me today," Walter said into the microphone. Unbeknownst to him, his old friend and mentor, Joshua O'Hare, was coming onto the stage from behind him. Josh held his finger to his pursed lips to let the audience know they should remain quiet as he sneaked up on his protégé. Walter sensed something was going on, but he did not know exactly what it was until he felt Joshua's hands over his eyes and heard his voice saying, "Guess who, Walter?" Immediately Walter spun around and the two men embraced as the audience laughed and cheered. The two greatest men that most of the Joshua's Tires managers had ever met were on the stage together before them, and the sight was powerful and motivating for all.

Josh took the microphone from Walter to give a brief tribute to his friend. "Walter, you make me proud every day!" he began. "This *positive passion* thing of yours is what I was searching for throughout my career. You have taken my little tire company and turned it into an icon of service and success that is respected all over the world. They will write books about you some day, Walt!" Walter bowed to Josh before lifting both hands in the air, pointing to Josh with his two index fingers to show the audience that they should be showing the greatest degree of attention and respect toward his mentor.

Turning again to the audience, Joshua put his arm around Walter's shoulder saying, "Let's have a final round of applause for this great man, and let's do it like we mean it!" With that, every person in the audience jumped to their feet and began applauding, cheering, yelling and whistling uproariously. Someone began chanting, "Walter and Joshua, Walter and Joshua." The entire audience joined in, all the while never slowing the applause. Josh, seeing that he had accomplished his goal, put the microphone down and the two men walked off stage with their arms draped over each other's shoulders. The significance of seeing the two leaders together was not lost on either Walter or Joshua, but they were still taken aback and humbled by the overwhelming support they had just received.

Genuine leaders never pursue or expect adulation or "star" status. When they receive it, they accept it graciously and move on to the next challenge. Leadership is not about personal victory. It is about winning through teamwork and positive energy by and for every member of the team.

SUCCESS

↑

POWER

↑

Opportunity
Sensitivity
Intelligence
Tolerance
Interest
Vision
Excitement

↑

POSITIVE PASSION

CHAPTER EIGHT

Personally Speaking

*Great men and women are all around us.
Most of them will never even be
aware of their own greatness...*

CHAPTER 8

Personally Speaking

After the leadership conference had ended for the day and the delegates were rushing to congregate outside the banquet hall for the evening's dinner, Walter was approached by a beautiful young lady he recognized from a tire dealers' convention he had attended in California two years prior. Brenda Considine was a journalist who wrote articles for the North American tire industry's most widely read trade journal. "Hi, Walter! It's great to see you again," she said enthusiastically.

"Well hi, Brenda. How are you? And what the heck are you doing here?" Walter asked with a smile.

"Actually, Joel and Bella invited me. They told me you would be giving a speech and that I might find it interesting enough to write an article on. I was in the room the whole time listening," she replied.

"Wow! Sorry I missed you. I generally like to make fun of the press when I see them in the audience while I am giving a speech," he quipped with a laugh. "So what did you think?"

"Walter, I have one word to describe it: great!" she said without hesitation. "I have never been to a tire industry conference where the CEO got up and gave a speech about positive thinking before. Usually they just get up and drone on about sales results and industry statistics. Then they generally like to pour out endless platitudes about how their company would be nothing without the employees. During those types of speeches I usually notice the people in the audience giggling and talking among themselves because they have heard it all before and don't believe a word of it. Yours was very different, Walter, and you really sold your concepts to your team. Personally speaking, I found it inspirational, and it was obvious that everyone else did too."

"Thanks a lot, Brenda. I am glad you liked it. I have always thought you have a lot of integrity as a journalist, and your approval means a lot to me," Walter said genuinely.

"So here is my idea, Walter. Let's you and I get together and do a series of articles about personal development and teamwork. I think we could come up with some great articles for trade publications of all kinds. There is no doubt in my mind that your concepts will work in any industry, and I think you should share your great views on positive thinking with everyone. It might even work into a book deal. What do you think?" Brenda asked with obvious excitement.

Walter thought for a moment and then said, "I am really busy doing my day job, Brenda, and I only did that speech today because Joel and Bella asked me to. I am not really in the freelance coaching or motivational speaking business. There are lots of professional speakers and authors out there doing just that already. Why don't you get one of them?"

A Passion for Leadership

"Because none of them are you, Walter! You are the real deal. You speak from the heart and you speak with experience. You are the most hands-on CEO I have ever met, and I know from speaking with many of your managers and staff over the years that you are the most beloved CEO in the business. There is no business coach or motivational speaker in the world who can bring the sense of reality to speaking and writing that you do. I am not leaving here until you say yes!" Brenda deliberately planted her feet and stared directly into Walter Kennedy's eyes as a big smile began to form at the corners of his lips.

"Man O Man, Brenda. You make a great case. Maybe you should be doing the motivational speaking!" Walter said before laughing out loud. "Okay, give me a call at my office on Monday and I will set aside some time to meet with you."

"That's great!" Brenda squealed before throwing her arms around Walter and giving him the hug of a lifetime. As she walked away, she had a skip in her step and a motion to her body that spoke volumes about her level of excitement and anticipation. In the months and years to come, she would have even more reason to be excited.

* * *

When Brenda arrived at Walter's office, Karla greeted her with a steaming cup of coffee and a warm smile. "One sugar with a touch of cream?" Karla asked.

"How did you know?" Brenda asked incredulously.

"Well, in all honesty, it is a little service trick that I do. Whenever Walter asks me to book an appointment, I do some research to find out what the visitor likes. I called your office and talked to your assistant,

Jennifer. She told me how you like your coffee in the morning but that in the afternoon you prefer sparkling water. You never eat donuts but you love heated muffins with butter. I will bring your muffin in when I get Walter his glazed donut in a few minutes. Oh, and please don't be mad at Jennifer. I swore her to secrecy," Karla said with obvious enthusiasm in her voice.

"Wow, Karla! This kind of thing just excites me. Walter doesn't only talk about **positive passion**, he is surrounded by it! Every time I meet a Joshua's employee, they seem to go the extra mile. You all appear happy, you all love working here, and most importantly, it is clear that you all love Walter. So what's the secret?" Brenda asked.

"No secret, Brenda. Walter is a very special guy, and I guess we all want to make him happy. We do little things to help him with his job. He is busy helping others all the time, so he deserves it. None of what I do is very difficult, and it only takes a second, but people seem to like it and Walter is always proud when his visitors compliment him on the service here," Karla said, beaming with pride.

Suddenly, Walter appeared at the doorway to his office saying, "Hey, Brenda! Right on time! I like that. I see you got your coffee. Is it just the way you like it?"

"It's perfect, Walter. Karla is treating me like royalty," Brenda said with a smile.

With that Karla walked briskly down the hallway to get a hot buttered muffin and a fresh glazed donut. Walter showed Brenda into his office, and for the next few minutes the two sipped on coffee and nibbled on their donut and muffin while making small talk about Walter's presentation at the annual management conference. Finally, when he thought the time was right, Walter said, "Okay, Brenda, tell me about your plan for our writing. I have some ideas of my own, but I am dying to hear what you have to say. I have given it a lot of thought, and I am actually quite excited."

"Oh, that's so great, Walter. Here is what I have in mind. I have my regular column in the *Tire and Brake* magazine that I can use as a launching pad for publicity in other magazines. I have an agreement with my publisher that I can freelance with other publishers as long as I provide a minimum amount of material for *Tire and Brake*. Frankly, there isn't much money in writing industry articles, so I have been supplementing my income with other articles for several years now. With the current North American management environment leaning toward personal development, I think you and I can come up with some very good articles, and as I said at the conference, we might even find a book deal in it. Oh, and I would like to end each article with the line **Positive passion creates success**. I think that would give us a theme for our series of articles," Brenda finished, and she looked into Walter's eyes for approval.

"Sounds good to me, Brenda. I will support you as much as I can. I was thinking about an article on self-awareness. I don't believe that anyone can ever be fully evolved, effective and passionate unless they understand themselves and how their actions impact other people. No one can ever have **positive passion** unless they can get beyond their own self-limiting tendencies. If they don't see themselves for what they really are, their presentation to others will not be genuine and probably won't be very effective. What do you think about that?" Walter asked.

Brenda's head was down and she had already started writing in her notebook. "Keep talking, Walter. This is great stuff. I will just keep taking notes until our time is up and then I will go back to my office and write the article. Once I have it polished, I will email it over to you for a final edit and then I will submit it for our next issue. The byline will read "by Brenda Considine and Walter Kennedy." Unless, of course, you would prefer that your name went first. What are your thoughts on that?"

"That sounds fine. You are the writer so your name should go first. So shall I just tell you what I think about self-awareness?" Walter asked.

"Yes, please. Keep talking." Brenda said almost impatiently.

The next two hours flew by as Walter talked and Brenda took notes. She was thoroughly impressed with Walter's depth in the area of human emotions and relationships. When her time was up, Brenda had taken thirteen pages of notes and could hardly wait to get back to her office to turn it into a feature article.

As promised, the article came out a few weeks later with Brenda and Walter in the byline together. Even though Walter had read the final draft and made some minor editorial changes, he was compelled to read it again in the summer edition of *Tire and Brake Magazine*. He smiled as he read. He was happy with the result.

In the years to come many articles would emanate from the writing duo of Brenda and Walter.

CHAPTER NINE
The First Article
SELF-AWARENESS

If you do not know yourself, you cannot truly know anyone else...

CHAPTER 9

The First Article

SELF-AWARENESS
The secret to effective leadership
by Brenda Considine and Walter Kennedy

Employers in the twenty-first century are facing challenges that the world of business management has never seen before. As the Baby Boomers retire, we will soon face a critical and overwhelming labor shortage. The Boomers and their children chose not have as many children as their parents did, and employers are now on the verge of actually having far more jobs than people to fill them. Voracious corporate appetites for increased production and financial growth must be fueled by a continuous supply of good quality candidates for employment. There will be some casualties in the fight for good workers, and the weak will not survive for long. Those employers who invest time, effort and resources in sophisticated employee recruitment, development and maintenance programs will prevail in the brave new world. It should be the goal of every business to become **The Employer of Choice** in their field if they want to survive.

There are thousands of companies and individuals in North America and abroad in the business of leadership training and development. You can hire them at great expense to come into your place of business and train you and your staff to work together more effectively and efficiently. You can have them teach personal development theory and better communication methodology. Some will teach customer service techniques and others will teach confrontation skills along with attitude adjustment lessons. Some will offer personality testing and individual employee reviews, while yet others will provide executive coaching and personal coaching for your workers. You name it and you can have it...for a price! The ranks of the gurus of human communication and business development are growing daily. Leadership training is a multi-billion dollar business, and it shows no sign of diminishing in the near future.

What employers sometime fail to understand or accept is that there is no magic pill or silver bullet to repair their staffing woes. Once the hired-gun leadership gurus have left their premises, organizations are on their own to maintain a positive, happy workplace loaded with loyal, efficient workers. Bosses need to understand that it is they and they alone who can make their business successful. People who sit in positions of authority need to realize that all eyes are on them. They are on stage twenty-four hours a day, seven days a week, and they need to be able to communicate and bond with the people that work for them. They must be beyond reproach, and they must understand the needs and wants of their employees. For today's workers, a job is not a privilege. It is a right, and if they don't like the job they have or the boss they work for, they can simply get another one. If the actions, attitudes or vision of the boss is not acceptable to the employees, that business may find itself in the ranks of the forgotten sooner than expected. **Today's employers must be great leaders.** There is no longer a place in business for despots, dictators, or absentee overseers. Bosses must work side by side with their employees, and they must never take them for granted. They must show that they care, and they must always dispense their favor and discipline fairly and consistently. They must understand that no matter how good their products are or how many years they have been a household name in the hearts of their customers, without a strong, loyal workforce they have nothing.

In order to be a great leader, an individual must understand his or her own personality and motivations. They must know and understand how they affect others and how well or how poorly they present themselves in each and every situation. Bosses must know themselves better than they know anyone else on the planet if they expect to succeed. Self-awareness is the key to effective leadership, and it resides in the soul of all great leaders, past and present. In the words of Walter

Kennedy, *"The difference between mediocrity and greatness is self-awareness."*

An amazing but all too common human trait is that most people really have very little idea of how others view them. They have a vision of themselves that is irrefutable, and they often believe that their view is the universally accepted view. It is also surprising how some people continue to pass along insults, slights, and simple rudeness day in and day out, oblivious to the fact that they are losing the respect of more and more people every day. People in authority often believe that their motivations, behaviors, and attitudes are the best, and in some cases, the *only* way to live and work. They make the assumption they are right, and therefore anyone who disagrees with them must be wrong. Some also believe that they worked hard to become the boss and now they have the *right* to make unreasonable demands while forcing their personal agenda on everyone in their employ. Some believe that respect should be automatic for a person in authority and that they have an indestructible lock on employee loyalty. That attitude might have worked in the days when there were more workers than jobs, but in the twenty-first century, such egocentric, regressive thinking will simply not work. Today's employees only respect employers who work hard to earn their respect daily, and they are only loyal to employers they feel strongly positive about. Strangely, many bosses think they are effectively expressing compassion, kindness and fair treatment because they give out an occasional bonus or make some great promises during a speech or in a corporate communication even though their day-to-day actions would indicate a complete lack of compassion. From these people, even positive reinforcement and complimentary emissions are usually rejected as some sort of management ploy. People in positions of authority are often oblivious to their own shortcomings and cannot see how repugnant they are to the people around them.

"So how does one discover self-awareness?" you ask. "And how does one know if the awareness they find actually represents what other people see and feel?" you might worry. The answer is quite simple. Ask someone! Every person should have a personal coach to help them understand how their actions affect others. Your personal coach is not there to tell you how to do your job. She is there only there to motivate you to better behavior by discussing any potential flaws, shortcomings, or warning signs they might see. That coach can be anyone from a co-worker to an outside consultant to your spouse. However, the person chosen must be emotionally able to provide an impartial, detached opinion. She must also be able to be honest in the toughest of situations where difficult or hurtful things must be said. It is important that you accept what your coach is saying and that you do not take anything personally. You must provide your coach with an environment of trust and safety. He or she must believe they can speak their mind without fear of harm or retribution. Conversely, your coach must be a person of the highest character, someone you trust implicitly to always speak honestly, and who consistently has your best interests at heart. Once you have selected your coach and he has agreed to help you, rely on him to be the window to your consciousness and your soul. Every time you fail to get a favorable reaction from someone, explain the situation to your coach and ask him what might have gone wrong. She won't always be right, but she will give you an impartial second opinion based on her view rather than yours. Your coach can also be useful as a sounding board for ideas and concepts that you plan to introduce to your workplace. Again, he can provide an impartial point of view to help you make the ideas palatable to others.

Another useful tool to assist with finding self-awareness is a personality assessment instrument. There are a number of assessment programs on the market today. Most are available online, and the survey and response times are extremely short. Despite their relative ease and speed of completion, these tests can provide valuable insight into your motivators, behaviors and natural skill levels in various areas. The information they provide is based strictly on your personal response to a series of questions, so in essence you are completely and personally responsible for the results. Once you have taken the assessment survey, have the report professionally reviewed so that you understand it fully, then give a copy of it to your coach. Because your coach will have a detached view of your motivators, behaviors and skills, they may be better equipped to accept the results of the assessment and utilize it to analyze why you might react in a particular way to a particular stimulus. They may also be able to warn you off from situations that will be unpleasant or difficult for you within the confines of your natural tendencies.

Since people tend to want to see the best in themselves, your coach can act as your alter ego and let you know when you are being rude, disrespectful, abrupt, arrogant, inconsistent or unreliable. They can also monitor your social awareness levels and warn you of inappropriate humor, inappropriate touching, talking down to others, obvious lying, or making promises you can't keep. With constant reminders and practice anyone can improve their self-awareness. Ultimately and ideally, the result will be that your social behavior and leadership skills will improve dramatically. When those skills become evident to your employees, any positive reinforcement or complimentary behavior that you employ will be accepted and appreciated.

The bottom line in your search for self-awareness is self-honesty! To be aware of yourself, you must be honest with yourself. There are probably a number of things that have left you unfulfilled or dissatisfied during your life. The chances are they were things you either had no skill in or were instances where you completely mishandled the situation. You might have allowed yourself to move past those situations by blaming someone or something else. Have the courage now to face up to your own shortcomings and take responsibility for your own actions. Accept that you are not an expert in *everything* and be aware that there are many areas in your life that could stand improvement. Allow yourself the luxury of being wrong occasionally and accepting the fact that you don't have to carry the weight of the world on your shoulders. Once you have committed to the fact that you are not perfect and there will always be areas where you can use help, you will be on the path to self-awareness. Once you gain a greater level of self-awareness and allow yourself to be vulnerable, you will be much better equipped to deal with the huge concept of becoming **The Employer of Choice** in your industry. You will never achieve *positive passion* until you achieve self-awareness.

Open yourself up to self-awareness and give yourself the option of becoming a great leader!

BC & WK

Positive passion creates success.

CHAPTER TEN

Article Two
MANAGEMENT DISENGAGEMENT: A TRAGEDY

"Manager" is another word for human being…

CHAPTER 10

Article Two

MANAGEMENT DISENGAGEMENT: A TRAGEDY
Do unhappy managers hate their jobs...or their companies?
by Brenda Considine and Walter Kennedy

We are often told that the majority of employees in North America quit their jobs due to dissatisfaction with their immediate superior rather than dissatisfaction with their job or their paycheck. It is true that most people feel the need to be appreciated, and yes, even *liked* by their supervisor or manager. However, in today's world more and more employees feel that the companies they work for must live up to the expectations of the people who work there. There is a feeling that corporations must have a social conscience and that the executive management teams must pay close attention to the feelings and emotional needs of its workforce. In the course of researching this subject, we also found that the higher employees climbed in the hierarchy of their companies, the more likely it was they would suffer from what we have now dubbed **management disengagement.** It is apparent that supervisors, managers, and even highly paid vice presidents are not exempt from the disease of management disengagement.

Walter Kennedy had the pleasure of interviewing two senior managers of Universal Mutual Funds of Hartford, Connecticut, on the subject of employee disengagement. What he found and what he was not prepared for was that even these two hard working managers carry a significant level of disengagement from their employers. *Note: We have changed their names in order to maintain confidentiality.*

John Williams is the Senior Sales Manager in the Hartford head office. Beverly Pearson is John's counterpart as Senior Operations Manager in the same office. We chose them as interview candidates because Walter knew them both to be extremely diligent and successful managers who had a reputation for fair play and integrity. They are well liked by virtually everyone who works for them, but despite all their accomplishments and popularity at Universal Mutual Funds, they are unhappy. When we called to ask them to participate in our research on disengagement, they both indicated a desire to speak with us - not because they wanted to talk about the disengagement of their employees, but because they wanted to speak about their own disengagement. Walter's interview follows:

Walter: "So John, I have known you for more than twenty years. I know you are the first person into the office in the morning and the last one out at night. Everyone knows you are totally dedicated to your staff, and your customers brag about the great service you and your team provide. You are revered in the mutual funds industry, and by all accounts you are at the top of your game. Not exactly the picture of disengagement that I am accustomed to. Why do you feel disengaged?"

John: "I guess it is safe to say that I am not disengaged from my job, Walter. I love my job and I love my staff. My people are the reason that I keep showing up here everyday. I am just not comfortable with Universal anymore."

Walter: "Okay. So I understand that you love your job, love your staff and are determined to come to work everyday. What has Universal done to make you so unhappy? Is it leadership? Is Bill James, the CEO, the problem?"

John: "Well, Bill is the captain of the ship so I suppose he is at least partially to blame, but I can't say that it is all about him. He has a job that nobody else really wants and he works very hard. No, Walter, I would have to say it is not the captain exclusively. It is the ship itself. Let me explain. Like so many companies, this one was originally created as a small local firm. In those days it was called Peterson Mutual Funds. Over the years partners were taken in and the business continued to grow. Eventually we acquired a lot of competing firms, then merged with Universal which was set on becoming the largest mutual funds brokerage firm on the continent. We are not quite there yet, but everyday brings us a little closer to reaching that goal. When I joined the firm twenty-two years ago, Bob Peterson was still here as my CEO, and boy, did we have a lot of fun. In those days the business was smaller and everyone took a lot of pride in working here. Bob ran the firm like he still owned it, and we all worked extra hard to make him happy. When Bob retired, things changed."

Walter: "What changed, John?"

John: "It became apparent that if we were going to become the largest funds broker on the continent, we would have to change the way we did business. The changes we made to work flows and process also caused segmentation and division of work groups. Many staff members who had worked side by side for years were no longer even working in the same building. Senior managers and supervisors were being transferred around the company on a regular basis, so there was really no continuity of management anywhere. When someone showed promise as an expert at something, they were immediately targeted for promotion or transfer, and again, work groups were split up. Growth-based promotions began to cause animosity among employees and managers alike because various folks felt that some of the promotions were not merited. I have to agree with that, Walter. We were grabbing some real under-achievers out of the staff pool and promoting them just because they had taken a correspondence course in something or gotten a certification in something else. Of course there were the usual patronage appointments as well. We learned very quickly that friends promoting friends is never a good idea, but strangely, it still happens today. At the same time, we were overlooking some really good people because of old movies or simply because we didn't know they existed. We were desperate for growth and we were making some bad decisions."

Walter: "That all sounds pretty bad, John. How did these growth symptoms affect morale?"

John: "It's been awful. We have lost some of our best people, and we continue to lose them to this very day. The people that were passed over felt that there was no room for them at Universal and they made the decision to move on to greener pastures. It kind of makes me laugh, but ironically some of those under-achievers who were promoted to better jobs left us too. Either they finally realized they did not have the skills to function in their new jobs, or the other staff chased them off. As much as we have had phenomenal growth, we have also had phenomenal brain-drain, and I sometimes wonder how big and how great we would be if we had all of those good people back. We have some awful people in management positions now, and nobody seems to know what to do about it. Bill, our CEO, and the executive management team are so busy working *on* the business that they have lost touch with what is going on *in* the business."

Walter: "So it sounds like what you are saying is that the members of the executive team at Universal have forgotten their roots and have lost touch with their best people."

John: "That's it in a nutshell, Walter. Morale is at an all time low, and I really don't know how long we can continue to grow or even survive with the problems we have, and it makes me very sad. I come here everyday hoping things will change. But they don't, so all I do is put in time working very hard while I wait for my pension or another opportunity. As much as I am compelled to work hard for my people and our customers, I just don't enjoy getting out of bed everyday. To make things worse, I am compelled to put on a brave face and tell my staff and my customers how great things are at Universal. I feel like such a hypocrite some times."

Walter: "So why don't you leave, John? Is it because of loyalty to the company?"

John: "No, it sure isn't loyalty that holds me back. Frankly, I get paid very well to do what I do, and after all of these years I find the work easy. Let's not forget that I have a great pension plan, too. At my age, I am not a hot commodity in the employment line, so it is simply very convenient for me to stay. I guess you could say that I am shackled by the chains of security. Besides, Walter, I really do love the people that work for me. I feel a real sense of obligation to stay and protect them. That's why I work so darned hard, too. I don't want to let them down."

Walter: "What about you, Beverly?"

Beverly: "Well, Walter, it is safe to say that I agree with everything John said but I have some additional, personal reasons for feeling the way I do."

Walter: "I would love to hear them, Bev."

Beverly: "I guess it all comes down to the fact that like so many other companies in the world, Universal only pays lip service to equality. And yes, I *am* talking about gender equality. This company is still run by men, and women are still treated like lesser citizens. I am so weary of watching men race to the top of the ladder while the women are at the bottom holding the legs so the men don't fall off."

Walter: "You are aware that you are a senior manager, aren't you, Bev?"

Beverly: "Of course I am, Walter. But have you ever wondered *why* I am a senior manager? Did you ever notice that I am only one of two female senior managers in the company?"

Walter: "Touché, Bev. So why do you think that is? Are you saying that Universal Mutual is run by a bunch of male chauvinists?"

Beverly: "I don't know if anyone on our executive management team actually understands what male chauvinism is. I think they think that by making me a senior manager, they have done their part to advance the cause of women in the workplace and that it is all they need to do. I am really a token woman here, Walter, and my voice counts for very little."

Walter: "Why do you say that, Bev?"

Beverly: "Well, as much as I was very pleased and happy to have been promoted to senior management, I soon learned that I was only senior in terms of my specific duties. Yes, I am in charge of my area, and yes, I must create the results that will make my department successful. In addition to that, I have to give reports to the executives on our business plans and progress, and I have to appear at official company functions. However, when the real decisions are made over a glass of scotch in the CEO's office, all I see are four or five men in there. When the executives have their nights out to sporting events, or weekends fishing, or impromptu poker games after work, I am not on the guest list. After they have their *men's club* meetings, they triumphantly announce how, after some intense research, they have decided to change the direction of the company. I never have a voice in any of those decisions, and frankly, I am tired of it.

What the executives in this company fail to understand is that all the members of the team must line up on the field at the same time for every game. They can't choose to have a woman player but only let her pinch hit when they feel like it. I am a full-fledged senior manager, and I want to be treated like one. I think they feel that I should stick to female management things, but what they don't realize is that there is no such thing. We all have the same job to do, and if they are going to advance women to senior positions, they need to understand that we want to be able to do everything that the men do.

Besides my own dissatisfaction, I have become a bit of an unwitting icon with the rest of the female staff here; you know, one of very few women who made it to the top. Because of that, I am expected to be a voice for the women. That is not happening either. My opinions and ideas are not taken seriously, and that is becoming evident to the majority of the female staff. If I advance ideas that are important to women, I am considered a women's libber and nobody listens. It is clear that I will never have an opportunity to advance to the CEO position in this company simply because I am a woman. However, I actually believe that becoming the CEO should be just as possible for me as it is for any of my male counterparts.

You asked me if the executive team is a bunch of male chauvinists. No, I don't think they are. They show great respect for women and readily admit that women have contributed greatly to the success of our firm. They simply don't understand that the world has changed and that women *are* truly equal. As John suggested, they are out of touch with their senior people and have no idea what we are thinking. They are lacking in social awareness and they appear to believe that they have all the good ideas."

Walter: "I will ask you the same thing I asked John. Why don't you leave?"

Beverly: "I will as soon as I find a better job. Like John, I am paid quite well, and I have a lot of friends here. I work hard for my team, and I don't want to let them down. I also put in a lot of hours here, and honestly, I do it to show the rest of the staff that I am devoted to my job and to them. I don't want to show disinterest or weakness because I am afraid that the overall morale would get even worse if I stopped trying. However, I am now mentally and emotionally committed to moving on, so it is just a matter of time before I cut the cord, so to speak. Besides, I am not disengaged from my job. I love my job. I am disengaged from Universal Mutual."

Walter: "Do you feel any loyalty at all to Universal Mutual?"

Beverly: "No, I don't. I feel great loyalty to my people, but as far as the firm goes, I feel nothing that could be described as loyalty. That makes me sad too. I have been here for over fifteen years, and I really wish I could say that I am intensely loyal, but I am not."

Walter: "One final question for both of you. What will it take to make you happy again?"

John: "I guess it comes down to communication, Walter. That and positive action. Our company needs to start listening to all of us, from the receptionist to the top level managers. We need an environment where good ideas are not the monopoly of the executives, and the executives need to understand what their people are feeling. It seems pretty simple to me, but at the same time it feels quite hopeless."

Beverly: "Yes, I am feeling that hopelessness too. I sometimes wish I could just run away. However, if I could get through to the executives that I am really equal to them and that I have some great ideas that can help the entire company, and if they listened to me and included me in *all* of their meetings, I would probably make a long term commitment to this company."

Walter: "Thanks to you both."

These two senior managers are typical of many we have met in the course of our research on employee disengagement. Their reasons for disengagement are different, but their feelings of despair are the same. Reduced loyalty and increased dissatisfaction of senior employees is becoming more common with each passing day. The tragedy in all of this is that without the unfailing support of its senior people, no company can remain strong or even viable for very long.

Positive action and positive reinforcement are absolutely imperative at all levels. You must practice **positive passion** with everyone in your employ. Do not assume that because your senior people are well paid and have been with you for a long time that they are happy or will always be there. Just because your top people are well liked and work hard every day, do not assume they are devoted to you. Any one of them could empty their desk and be gone tomorrow. Talk to them. Ask them what they want. Make sure that every one of them is an active and important member of your team. Most importantly, treat them equally and fairly. **Management disengagement** is a very real and a very contagious disease. If you don't believe us, just go down to one of the local watering holes in your own town after work one day and ask a few people in business suits how happy they are at work.

BC & WK

Positive Passion creates success.

CHAPTER ELEVEN
Article Three
POSITIVE CONSISTENCY

If I am fair to everyone, we all win...

CHAPTER 11

Article Three

POSITIVE CONSISTENCY
Inconsistency is a killer disease to teamwork.
by Brenda Considine and Walter Kennedy

So you have gone to college, achieved a degree and found your dream job. You have committed Steven Covey's, *Seven Habits* to memory, and you have listened to every CD that Tony Robbins ever made. You have moved into a management job and are now officially a *leader*. But do you know what leading is all about? Do you know what those you lead expect of you? Are you an effective leader or just a mediocre manager?

You must never assume that a title such as manager, sales leader, supervisor or vice president will get you the respect of your team or improve the results of your department. Employees of the twenty-first century are not at all impressed by titles. They are only impressed by the actions of those who lead them. The thing that is most likely to make you successful as a leader is your own ability to be the best you can be at all times. In this article we will explore some of the things that will convince your employees that you are doing your personal best and that you have **positive passion** for each and every one of them.

There is an overused expression that originated in the movies that applies extremely well to leadership. That expression is, "You can talk the talk, but can you walk the walk?" If you want to gain credibility with your employees, you must be able to walk the walk every day. You must first understand that your employees actually *need* a leader to guide them. Teams without coaches and platoons without sergeants generally do not exist in our culture, and there are good reasons for that. Human beings need a central figure to carry the vision of the team and supervise the actions necessary to make it successful. That is an irrefutable fact of life. Over the course of human history, the best teams and most successful armies have been directed by the very best leaders. Leadership has been proven to be the deciding factor in human success time and time again. To be an effective and revered leader, you must know your business and you must be able to give intelligent, well thought out direction to your team every step of the way. Most importantly, you must be there to assist them in accomplishing the things you want done. Don't make the mistake of assuming you can give directions at a meeting once a year, or even once a month, and then lock yourself in your office until the next meeting. Coaches and sergeants are in the stadium and on the battlefield consistently all day, every day. Their teams need to know their leader is a part of the team who has as much to lose and as much to gain as everyone else. The secondary benefit to this is that when leaders are present, they have the opportunity to *inspect what they expect* every day and make recommendations and adjustments when issues appear.

The most trusted and revered leaders are the most consistent and reliable leaders. They are the ones who walk the walk. Even though they are flexible and will listen to many points of view, when they make a decision, they stand by it. When they say they are going to do something, they move heaven and earth to get it done. These are the men and women who become captains of industry and have the respect of everyone around them. They work diligently at all times and they have solid principles. They set the example for industriousness for their team and never allow sloth or dishonesty to overcome them. Open, honest communication is the *only* way to communicate in their world. They are not afraid to admit when they are wrong, and they will accept criticism without retaliation. They will learn from their mistakes, and they will work tirelessly for the good of the team. Unfortunately, many leaders assume they have the trust and respect of their teams when they do not, and they cannot understand why they are failing. This is a common symptom of a condition called *lack of social awareness*. Leaders with this condition simply do not have the basic ability to read people or comprehend the telltale signs of dissatisfaction.

Leaders must be extremely cognizant of their own attitudes. That, too, must be consistent. Leaders cannot be happy one minute and angry the next. Leaders may not publicly criticize or shun an employee on Thursday, then give them a performance award on Friday. It takes the average person approximately nine positive situations to emotionally overcome one negative event. Because of that statistic, bad leaders seldom have the opportunity to recover from negative acts against employees. Real leaders will never show anger toward a team member, and they will not allow themselves the luxury of self-pity. Leaders must be stable in their emotions and strong in their resolve. Team members need to know that their leader is a *rock*, a person who is always able to come to their rescue and who is always able to make a rational decision. There is no room in business for leaders with stress, leaders with depression, or leaders with anger management problems. People with those issues are simply *not* leaders. Interestingly and importantly, real leaders tend to smile more often than they frown.

Leaders must always pay attention to the concerns and desires of their team members. They must be on the field, paying attention and showing interest in their team members at all times. They must act when they are aware of problems or challenges, and they must treat each employee with the same degree of respect. Equal treatment of employees is extremely important. No business in this century may succeed when any sort of class system is in place. Every job is integral to the success of every business, and since the business cannot operate without every person in every position, it follows that they all have an equal level of value. Of course it is true that highly skilled jobs where a greater level of training or education is required will usually garner a larger compensation package, but that does not mean that highly skilled employees should be treated with a greater level of respect than those who are paid less. Leaders must always recognize that there is no room in modern business for discrimination on the basis of gender, race or religion, and that even casual humor in that regard is not appropriate in the workplace.

Be careful how you dispense your attention and your favor. It is an all too true fact that "the squeaky wheel gets the grease," but it can also be the best way to disengage employees. No one likes a teacher's pet, and no one likes to see attention and favors showered lavishly upon one employee while others are virtually ignored or only tolerated. You should never provide perquisites or promotions based on friendship, and any personal relationships you have outside the office should be left at the door when you go to work each day. Be careful of employees who spend a lot time praising you and hanging around when they have no reason to be involved. Those people often have ulterior motives for their apparent fascination with you, and they can be your eventual downfall. Even if you have a particularly talented and successful employee, only acknowledge and reward them for the specific actions or events for which they are responsible. Use their success as encouragement to others, but do not put them on a permanent pedestal. That kind of idolatry will be completely disengaging for the majority of your team. If they believe they will never be acknowledged because they can never be as successful as your idol, they will stop trying. Every employee does *something* good from time to time, and they all deserve acknowledgement and positive reinforcement as often as possible.

Positive consistency in people management is one of the most powerful leadership tools you have available to you. If your employees trust you and respect you for fairness at all times, they will work tirelessly to create success for you and for their team.

If you believe you are failing as a leader or have not gained the degree of success you desire, give yourself a consistency check.

1. **Do you control your emotions at all times?**

2. **Do you practice smiling instead of frowning?**

3. **Do you work hard at all times?**

4. **Do you give equal and fair treatment to all employees?**

5. **Do you really listen to all points of view?**

6. **Do you accept that every job is important?**

7. Do you appear on the playing field every day?

8. Do you have an awareness of your own attitudes?

9. Do you know whether or not your employees respect you?

10. Do you *walk the walk* all day, every day?

If you answered NO to any of these questions, you have an opportunity to improve your leadership skills and create greater success for you and your team.

BC & WK

Positive passion creates success.

CHAPTER TWELVE

The Natural Tendency of Human Beings

No man has the right to harm another in any way....

CHAPTER 12

The Natural Tendency of Human Beings

After a series of very well received articles, Walter and Brenda garnered a great deal of attention from the publishing industry. Before they knew it, they were offered a book deal. Walter was not sure he was ready to write an entire book, but Brenda convinced him that he owed it to the world to share his ideas in a bigger way. Although he would not admit it to her, Walter secretly really liked the idea of seeing his name on a book jacket.

"So now that you have talked me into this book deal, what the heck are we going to write about?" Walter asked with a grin.

"I think first we need to sit down and come up with an outline. We need a roadmap to follow. Otherwise the book will spin out of control with disjointed thoughts and disconnected ideas," Brenda said seriously.

"Well, we can't have that!" Walter laughed. "So how do you think we should start?"

"Impress me, oh wise one," Brenda said with a smile. "I'm betting you have something on your mind that will get the ball rolling. Tell me what you have been thinking about lately."

"Hmmm. You know, I have been thinking about war lately," Walter stated.

"War! We aren't going to write a book about war are we? I don't think that's what the public is expecting, Walter!" Brenda asked fearfully.

"Calm down, Brenda. This is an interesting subject. I recently read an article which said that in 1968 two historians named Will and Ariel Durant calculated that in the previous 3,421 years of recorded history, there have only been 268 years without a war somewhere in the world. It also indicated that there has not been a single year since 1968 without a war somewhere on planet earth," Walter stated. "To me, war is the ultimate expression of man's inhumanity to man, and frankly, I am a little shocked that human beings think so little of mankind that they continually feel the need to kill each other in the most inhumane of ways. Just think of it, Brenda. People are killing each other in the name of politics, religion and territorial dominance somewhere in the world virtually every day of our lives. That tells me that human beings are fundamentally flawed in the sense that they believe conflict and violence are acceptable ways to resolve their differences. Are you beginning to understand where I am going with this?" Walter asked.

"Oh, yes. Now it is starting to make sense. Tell me more!" Brenda said excitedly.

"Okay, listen up. Think about this for a minute. You and I have written all kinds of articles about tolerance, understanding and positive thinking. This century has created a multi-billion dollar world wide industry of speakers, authors and business coaches who promote the concepts of communication and understanding. The churches and temples of the world are packed with peace loving people who seem to want everyone in the world to get along. Most people I meet in the course of my day want to believe that everyone should be kind and good to their fellow men and women. And yet, we continue to have wars…and lots of them! The only conclusion I can draw from all this is that mankind has a basic need to be fighting at all times. Take it a little further and think about sports." Walter stopped speaking because he could see that Brenda wanted to say something.

"So let me try to understand where we are going with this. We are going to write a book that blatantly states mankind is brutal and violent, and then we'll come up with a cure or a batch of various cures for the disease?" Brenda said slightly sarcastically.

"Something like that," Walter said with a smile. "Let me go on a bit so that I can pull my thoughts together. Think about sports. Boxing is a sport where grown men and women punch each other senseless while millions of people watch. As you know, the best way to win a boxing match is the knockout, which amounts to actually beating someone until they lose consciousness. People love to watch that happen. I find it odd that civilized people find boxing, wrestling, kick boxing or any of the martial arts to be *arts* at all. How can a deliberate attempt to harm another person until they are no longer able to defend themselves be considered an art? Even the less violent sports such as soccer, football and hockey contain occasional outbreaks of violence that drive spectators wild. They love it when a couple of grown men start swinging at each other during a game where the only object is to put a ball or a puck into a goal. Often it even stimulates them to the point where the violence on the field or on the ice is somehow transferred into the minds of the fans, causing fights to break out in the stands.

Think about politics. Politicians are a bunch of folks who think nothing of destroying the lives of their opponents if it suits their purposes, and if need be, they will start wars to make a point. People in democratic countries all over the world leave their homes on a regular basis to vote for politicians who they expect to uphold their rights and fight battles for them. If the politicians they elect start wars they believe in, the voters will support them. If they don't believe in a particular war, the voters will immediately turn on the very politicians they elected. Politics is kind of an indirect and safe way for everyone to get into serious conflict without getting hurt.

Take all of this a little further into the field of education. Spelling bees and debates in school are non-violent conflicts, but they are conflicts nonetheless. During those events, students are asked to study, practice and train for long periods of time in order to be more fit and able to *beat* the teams they must compete with. There is an element of competition that allows children to compete without physically harming each other. When the kids go out into the schoolyard at recess, they play marbles or hopscotch or other games that involve competition. Occasionally schoolyard fights break out even among the youngest children. If you think about it, most of the activities human beings share among each other involve an element of competition that is either violent or has the propensity for leading to violence.

Think even about love. How many times do we hear about married couples in violent disputes? How many times do we hear about two men fighting over the same woman or two women fighting over the same man? Conflict...conflict...conflict. Husbands and wives often fight about money, relatives, and their children. They fight because even between two people who love each other, there is a need to win. Hence, the alarming world divorce rate.

In business, Brenda, we have constant disputes with our competitors, our suppliers, our customers and, of course, among our employees. And that is where we come in," said Walter as he stopped to think.

Brenda felt the need to fill the silence. "Wow, Walter. I have never given much thought to it before, but you are right. People are in minor disputes and huge fights with other people all the time. Even reality shows are a form of conflict, and God knows that television is the best delivery system for violence the world has ever known. We can all watch genuine death and destruction in full color any time we want just by turning on the TV. This is big. I think we could write a series of books on this subject!" she said enthusiastically.

"Yes, I suppose we could write a series of books on war, Brenda, but I want to focus more on helping people to recognize their own negative tendencies and on teaching them how to practice ***positive passion***. I want our readers to understand that we don't need to fight and argue with our co-workers in order to make a point. I want them to know that bosses are not there to make their lives a living hell, and I want them to become more aware of the significance of their own actions. I want everyone to understand that when they have positive thoughts in their minds, they have an opportunity to spread that positivism to others and make the world a better place to live."

"Gotcha, Walter. So how should we start this book?" Brenda asked.

Walter sat back in his chair and thought for a second before saying, "Well, I am thinking that we should begin with some statistics about war and civil unrest and follow that with some discussion about the various violence and dispute issues that you and I have just discussed. I want to make it clear that human beings have a natural need for dominance and control over each other that cannot be denied. I want to follow it with the fact that as much as we accept that human beings have a competitive and sometimes violent nature, we can also be kind and compassionate whenever we choose to. We need to bring our readers to the concept of 24/7 understanding and thoughtfulness. We want them to understand that even though competition will and must exist in the business world, there is no place on our planet for violence among people and there is no need for conflict in the workplace. I want them to understand that loyalty is not automatic and that it must be earned by each and every person on an almost daily basis. ***Positive passion*** is not something that can be given to anyone. It can only be learned through conscious thought and continuous effort."

Feeling he had gotten his point across, Walter finished speaking and looked over at Brenda with a peaceful smile on his face. Brenda smiled back at him, secure and confident in the knowledge that she was about to co-author a great leadership book. And she was right. The book was an immediate commercial success and topped the New York Times bestseller list for over a year. That taste of success led to a series of highly successful books that would become a legacy for Walter Kennedy and the creator of financial freedom for Brenda Considine.

Positive passion creates success!

THE END FOR ME.

A NEW BEGINNING FOR YOU.

Wayne Kehl

www.waynekehl.com

AFTERWORD
Personal Vision

To be passionate "about" life we must discover our true passion "in" life

Afterword

As we wander through the short period of time that is our life, we make hundreds of thousands, or perhaps even millions of choices. We make so many choices in a lifetime that at the time just before our passing, we have forgotten all but the most significant of them. We remember our choice to marry and to whom; we remember our first job and what lead us to it; we remember our first drink of alcohol; we might forget our third lover and our second lover but we will always remember our first and last. The majority of our choices simply evaporate into invisible vapor like the morning dew.

The choices that are not easy to make are the most significant of all. Those choices are also the most difficult to reverse and the most heartbreaking when we recall them at the end of our lives. The hardest choices always involve our greatest inner passions. When we fail to follow our heart and pursue our true passion we create unrelenting regret and self-doubt. In time, one passion may be replaced with another, but we will always recall the passions we left behind and make excuses for our decisions not to pursue them.

We all have a personal vision that we dream of. That vision may change occasionally as the years pass, but as we drive down a highway or lay in bed sleeplessly at night, we are often consumed by our personal vision. We see ourselves as singers, musicians, policemen, fishermen, writers, millionaires, or kings. In our vision, we can be beautiful, handsome, sophisticated, and bold. We imagine trysts with beautiful women, or handsome strangers that we meet in passing; we imagine ourselves achieving an award for the great work we did on our latest work project or as the coach of our children's volleyball team. We envision ourselves winning a lottery or inventing something great. We might use our imaginary fortune to purchase a huge house in any country we choose, with a view of any vista we wish to see. Our personal vision is always better than the life we live because until we reach the age when we are mature enough to understand that we have reached our maximum potential, we want what we do not have. That is the nature of mankind and it is what created the world as we now know it. Many of the personal visions of the millions of people before us have become reality. If none of our forefathers had pursued their personal visions we might still be living in caves.

Human beings are humble, yet vain creatures. Despite the natural tendency of most people to avoid being significant above all others, we all need to be accepted and acknowledged from time to time. We need to be patted on the back and told that we are good, or even that we are the very best at *something*. A desire for acknowledgement consumes some people to the point that they make themselves universally disliked. Their overwhelmingly positive feelings for themselves often create negative feelings in others. And yet, there are people who are so afraid of attention from others that they live a life of misery…frightened that they might be singled out for praise, all-the-while yearning for it more than life itself. Both types of people need positive reinforcement and both need to be acknowledged and loved.

Bears, spiders, birds, and fish feel neither arrogance nor greed; neither pride nor hate; neither embarrassment nor disgrace. Only humans have emotions that are stimulated by communication with others of their own kind. Only humans can make a serious impact positively or negatively on members of their flock with a look or a sigh. Only humans can make one of their kind a success or a failure with just the will of a quorum. An alpha male wolf must enter into physical combat with all comers in order to rule the pack. There is positive energy in the fight but fortunately that model will not work for civilized human beings. Thanks to our intellect, we are able to find other ways to create positive results, without violence. We have the ability to move beyond instinct and use reason in order to transform palpable negativity into a positive result. ***Positive passion*** is what separates animals from human beings.

Always remember that as you follow your personal vision, another is following his and it is probably dramatically different from yours. Just as you cherish your vision, his vision must also be allowed to live. Everyone's personal vision is different and you must not try to force yours on someone else. Never allow the negativity of anyone, no matter how important they might seem, destroy your dream or pull you from the path you have chosen. Never attempt to dissuade others from their own personal visions as you will risk breaking their spirits or losing them altogether.

You cannot be passionate about something for which you feel no passion. You will never be truly successful with a mate you do not love and you will never be successful in a job you do not like. You will never achieve satisfaction with pure negative energy and you will not motivate others with constant negative reinforcement. If you think positively and exude positive energy while passionately following your personal vision, you will succeed beyond your wildest dreams and achieve happiness beyond your imagination.

In my personal vision, I see myself as a writer; an author of books on leadership. I have pure ***positive passion*** for my vision and while you are reading my book you are helping me reach my goal. My vision has materialized and I thank you for that.

I hope when you find your own personal vision, you will follow it relentlessly. Chase it like your life depends on it. You will never regret that choice.

Positive Passion Creates Success!

Wayne Kehl